# 101 Rock Climbing Tips and Tricks

Tips for Better Sport Climbing, Trad Climbing, Multi-Pitch Climbing, Rappelling, and More

By Tristan Higbee

Copyright © 2016 by Tristan Higbee. All rights reserved.

This book or any portion thereof may not be reproduced or used in any manner whatsoever without the express written permission of the author except for the use of brief quotations in a review.

All images are by the author unless otherwise noted.

Cover: A climber on *Blues Riff* (5.11b/c) on the Phobos/Deimos Cliff in Yosemite's Tuolumne Meadows. Photo by Greg Epperson.

Visit the author's websites at *http://theundercling.com* and *http://thealoof.com*.

ISBN: 978-0-9977460-2-0

---

DISCLAIMER

Climbing is dangerous. You can die. The tips written in this book are for educational purposes only. You must decide for yourself if something is dangerous or not. By reading further into this book, you acknowledge that you are taking things into your own hands and will not hold the author responsible for any accident or injury that may occur. Climb and apply these tips and tricks at your own risk.

# Contents

| | |
|---|---|
| Introduction | 5 |
| Essential Climbing Tips | 7 |
| General Climbing Tips | 21 |
| Sport Climbing Tips | 33 |
| Trad Climbing Tips | 39 |
| Multi-Pitch Climbing Tips | 55 |
| Gear Tips | 67 |
| Training and Downtime Tips | 85 |
| Rappelling Tips | 91 |
| Other Tips | 95 |

# Introduction

The content in this book is made up mostly of blog posts that I wrote over the course of a couple of years for a now defunct climbing blog. The tips are loosely sorted into categories, and each tip is its own bite-sized chunk of climbing knowledge.

I've been climbing for more than 18 years and have established around 200 new routes. The tips in this book come straight from my years of experience. Beginning climbers will find a lot of information here that will make their climbing lives a lot easier. Even if you're an experienced climber, I expect you'll find some tips here that you haven't heard or seen before.

If you'd like to tell me how much you loved or hated the book—or if you have any other questions, comments, or suggestions—feel free to contact me. I tweet about climbing news and tips at *@climbingtips*, write about stuff related to climbing at *http://theundercling.com*, and write about my other outdoor adventurs at *http://thealoof.com*.

Happy climbing,
Tristan Higbee

# Essential Climbing Tips

# 1. 3 Toproping Tips for Aspiring Leaders

I went climbing with a couple of relatively inexperienced friends not too long ago. They've both led before, but they're still in that stage where they toprope a lot. As I watched them toprope some climbs, several pointers came to mind. Below are the tips that I would give to aspiring or beginning leaders to help them get a more realistic idea of what to expect when leading.

**1. Pay attention to where the bolts are** – When you're leading, you climb where the bolts are. It's easy when toproping to deviate from "the line" of the route into easier or harder (or more dangerous) terrain. When on toprope, try to always stay within arm's reach of the bolts.

**2. Remember the consequences of falling** – Falling on toprope is not a big deal. At all. The rope stretches a bit, or you might take a swing if you're climbing too far off to the side, but that's it. When lead climbing, there are times when you just do not fall. Maybe you're above inadequate gear, or maybe there's a ledge below you that you'll break your ankles on if you fall. When on toprope, be sure that you're aware of what's around you. Think to yourself, "OK, if I were leading this, I really, really wouldn't want to fall here."

**3. Practice clipping or placing gear** – Letting go with one hand to clip a bolt or place a cam definitely makes leading harder. It's an important element that is missing when toproping. If you're TRing a sport route, think about where you'd clip from and then pretend to clip. One common practice is to simply touch the bolt hanger for a second. No, it's not the same as reaching down, unclipping a quickdraw from your harness, bringing it up, clipping it into the bolt, reaching down for the rope, bringing it up, and clipping it into the draw (phew!), but at least it's something. If you want a more realistic version, take quickdraws up with you and practice clipping.

Another option is to have the leader leave the draws clipped into the bolts so that you have to unclip them as you climb up on toprope. If you're on a single-pitch trad route, you can do the same thing; that is, you can have the leader leave his/her pieces of gear in the crack for you to remove as you climb up. Or you can just mentally note where and when you'd place the pieces. It's also useful to examine each gear placement, figure out why the leader placed it there, and assess whether it's a good placement.

# 2. Don't Put Your Leg in Front of the Rope When Leading

You're on a desperate lead and fighting to stay on. You're trying to get your fingers to close but your forearms are absolutely destroyed. You half-heartedly lunge for a hold, knowing that you'll probably take a fall. You start to drop. All of a sudden you're upside down. You've smacked your head on the wall and you're seeing stars. What happened?

The likely culprit? Your foot got in front of the rope. Figure 1 shows what I'm talking about (it's a view of the back of the climber).

Note that the rope is behind the climber's right leg. Go through in your head what would happen if this climber were to fall. Instead of falling normally, the rope going behind his leg would flip him upside down. Keep your leg behind the rope to avoid this scenario.

This is still something that even more advanced climbers struggle with from time to time. One way to get out of the bad habit (or any bad climbing habit, really) is for you and your partners to watch each other and call each other out when you see the dirty deed.

*Figure 1. The rope is behind the climber's right leg. Not good. (Tip #2)*

# 3. Should You Practice Falling?

Should beginning climbers take time to practice falling? Will this help them build confidence and overcome fear?

I think it really depends on each climber individually. Most beginning leaders have a healthy fear of falling, and that's natural. The question is, just how scared are you? If the idea of falling absolutely paralyzes you and keeps you from climbing anything even slightly above your comfort zone, then yes, I would recommend that you practice falling.

At first, just clip into a bolt and have your belayer take in all the slack. Let go so that you're supported by the rope. Then climb a little bit higher and let go. To be honest, I've never done any falling just for the sake of falling (my first falls just came naturally from sucking at climbing and being overly ambitious), so it'll be up to you to determine where your comfort zone is and how long of falls you are willing to take.

If you are going to practice falling, make sure you won't hit any ledges or other objects on your way down and that all falls will be clean. Vertical or overhanging walls are best for this unless you relish that cheese-grater-on-your-hands feeling.

If you haven't taken any falls because you lack climbing experience rather than having some kind of paralyzing fear, then I'd say just keep climbing. You'll fall eventually. If you've climbed up to 5.9 and haven't taken any falls, get on a 5.10. You'll either fall and realize that falling is not too bad, or you'll waltz right up the thing. Either way, it will be a good experience, right?

I have two more thoughts on this. First, if you don't want to fall, then don't! If you really are scared of falling and are happy on the routes you currently can send without falling, more power to you. Climbing is your game, and if you're happy the way you do it, don't let anyone tell you different. But that brings me to the second thought, and that is to keep in mind that falling really isn't too bad. Most of the time it's over before you even realize what's happening. The more you do it, the easier it gets.

Overall, I would recommend getting used to falling. Whether that entails actively practicing it or just falling from being on stuff that's too hard for you to climb is your prerogative. When you're not scared out of your gourd, you'll find it easier to focus on the climbing itself, and the whole experience becomes more enjoyable

# 4. Don't Rely Blindly on Guidebooks

A couple of years ago, a buddy and I had a somewhat unpleasant time on a route down in southern Utah that was inadequately described in the guidebook. The

"5.6, 100-foot" second pitch was more like a 5.9, 170-foot pitch. Also, the fixed anchors that the guidebook showed to be on top of the route were absent. On top of that, the descent information was bad too. "Walk off north, then down ledges at tip of formation" turned into class 4 and 5 downclimbing, a rappel, and more sketchy downclimbing and scrambling. Luckily we had enough time and experience that everything went fine. It was more inconvenient than anything else, but the inaccurate information could have gotten us in real trouble.

The moral of the story here is that while guidebooks are great, don't rely solely on them. Information there is often incomplete or even wholly inaccurate. Guidebook authors are human too. Look at beta online and in other guidebooks (if there is more than one guidebook to the area). Ask people about the route. And just take a good, long look at the route. That's probably the most important thing. Look at the route! If we had taken the time to just look up at that route from the base, we would have easily seen that the second pitch was longer than the first (which was 100 feet long).

In other words, if you're looking for information about a climb, do everything in your power to make sure it's the correct information. At the end of the day, though, it's up to you to not get lost or hurt. Don't blame it on the guidebook.

# 5. Knot the End of Your Rope

On that same trip to southern Utah, my belayer was witnessing an epic unfold next to him while I led the first pitch of a route. A group of climbers had arrived at the crag. One of them seemed to know what he was doing, but the three or four others didn't. The competent climber led off up a route and was lowered down after reaching the anchors. Well, the pitch was evidently longer than half of a rope length because as the climber was being lowered, the end of the rope slipped through the belayer's belay device! By some amazing stroke of luck, the climber was standing on a small ledge when it happened, and he didn't fall. He did have to make a tricky down-solo, though, to get back to the ground. This story was a hair's breadth away from having a very not-so-happy ending.

This is such a stupid way to get hurt, and there is such an easy way to prevent it. Simply tie a knot in the end of the rope. Both the belayer and the climber should each check to make sure there's a knot there before the climber starts off. The most common knot is the stopper knot (view step by step instructions at *http://www.chockstone.org/TechTIps/Stopper.htm*), but any solid knot will do, really. If you use a rope bag or tarp that has tie-in loops for each end of the rope, make sure the knot on the bottom end is solid enough that it can't come undone.

# 6. Climb For the Fun Of It

I climb a lot in the summer, and each summer I end up getting sick of climbing for a couple of weeks. Two summers ago, a friend and I were developing an area in a nearby canyon. He had work and family obligations; I had neither. As a result, I was up at the cliff every day building trails, cleaning lines, bolting lines, hauling gear, and so on. This went on for a couple of months. After a while, I was just sick of it. I hated the area. I hated bolting. I hated the mountains. I hated climbing. You know what they say about too much of a good thing, right? The problem wasn't that I was climbing every day; it's that I wasn't going up there every day for the right reasons. I was going up just to get stuff done, not necessarily because I wanted to go up there. It turned from play into work. And I think that's a really important thing to keep in mind. As a result of all this, I completely stopped climbing for about a month. I took that time off and returned to climbing with excitement and zeal that I hadn't felt in ages.

Yes, it is fun to, say, work sport routes... IF that's what you enjoy doing. Yes, it is fun to carry gear and build trails... IF you enjoy it. I've had a lot of friends get hardcore into climbing for a year or two and then just drop off the face of the earth. They climbed just to climb hard. I think they were limiting the fun they were having by feeling like they always had to be projecting something epic. I think they forgot about just having fun and enjoying the act of climbing for what it is.

Don't burn out. Climb because you love it, because you enjoy it. Don't let climbing become a chore. We all have enough of those already.

# 7. Trust Your Gut

There have been two trips in the last year that I planned on going on and then backed out of at the last minute. There have been a handful of routes I've gotten on in the last year that I've backed off of. For whatever reason, sometimes I just feel uneasy about certain trips or certain climbs. This could just be self doubt, nerves, over-analysis, an understanding of my own weaknesses, divine inspiration, or a number of other things, but why risk it? There have been times when I've ignored that feeling and regretted it (like when I nearly got killed by a car-sized piece of falling ice while ice climbing).

As you climb more and gain more experience, you'll learn what that gut feeling feels like and what it means. The route will always be there.

# 8. 9 Ways to Climb Better Without Even Trying

Psha. Forget spending all winter in the gym. Forget churning out a hundred pull-ups at a time. It turns out you don't even have to try to get better at climbing. Here are nine things you can do the next time you go to the crag that can help you pull down harder:

**1. Stretch** – Stretching warms up your muscles and prevents injury. You don't want to get a lactic acid pump right at the crux of your project. You don't want to miss that key high foothold just because your legs are stiff. And you definitely don't want to pull a muscle and have to sit out the rest of the season.

**2. Get a good night's sleep** – I'm still furious at the loud and annoying girls who stayed up talking all night in the campsite next to mine in Moab that one time. I was so tired the next day that I had to bail off of a big route I'd been really excited about for months. On a related note, make sure you don't do anything that would hinder anyone else's ability to get a good night's sleep.

**3. Be well fed and hydrated** – Have you ever bonked because you just don't have the energy? It's no fun. Make sure you've got enough fuel in your system to keep you going. Take food and water with you on longer routes.

**4. Warm up** – In addition to lubing and oiling your muscles, warming up on an easier route before jumping on one at your limit helps with getting you in the zone mentally.

**5. Have good gear** – If you're concerned as you climb above that ancient used cam you bought off eBay that it will hold if you fall off, your mind won't be focusing on the task at hand (i.e., not falling in the first place). Use gear that you're confident in.

**6. Know what you're doing** – If you're confident in your knowledge and abilities, you won't be distracted from the climbing at hand by worrying about what exactly it is you're supposed to do when, for example, you get to the anchors or to a long runout section.

**7. Climb with good people** – They don't necessarily have to be good climbers (although that helps too). Just climb with the people you enjoy being with and who get you excited about climbing.

**8. Minimize external distractions** – Leave the dog at home, turn off the cell phone, and avoid playing loud music.

**9. Have fun** – Haven't you heard that the best climber in the world is the one having the most fun? It's true. Don't take your route or yourself too seriously, and keep the climb in perspective. You're climbing a big rock, not solving world hunger.

## 9. Look Ahead

I did a very long (1,700-foot/518-meter) slab route a few years ago. The easiest pitches were only about 5.0 and 5.3. This meant that the climbing flew by, but there was a problem. This route had 200-foot (60-meter) runouts on these easy pitches—meaning potential 400-foot (120-meter) falls at the top of the pitches—so it was very important to not get off-route into looser rock and more difficult climbing. I had to keep reminding myself to look ahead to see where I was going, to see where the route went. I had to actively keep myself from looking solely at my feet and hands and not getting the big picture of the pitch. No one likes full rope-length, and even fewer survive them.

This advice also applies to single-pitch routes. You don't want to suddenly find yourself away from the line of bolts with no way to get back on track. Look ahead from each bolt or each gear placement to see where the next bolt or gear placement is.

In short, know where you're going and where the route is going. Don't get so caught up in the actual climbing, easy though it may be, that you climb straight into trouble.

## 10. Tell People Where You're Climbing

Whenever you're going climbing or hiking somewhere off the beaten path, it's not a bad idea to leave a note or tell someone where you are. If something goes wrong and you're not back by a certain time, people will know where to come looking for you.

This is especially important if you're going out alone. Remember Aaron Ralston, the guy who had to cut off his own arm because it became crushed under a boulder while he was canyoneering by himself? Think how different that story would have been if he had just left a note with someone.

My roommates in college got a nervous chuckle out of my leaving notes on the fridge that said things like, "Gone climbing in ____. Should be back Sunday night. If not back by Monday, call ____, because I'm probably dead or in trouble. I'm serious."

# 11. Think and Climb Accurately

One great way to waste your energy on a climb is to grope around for the right hold or just blindly reach for something you hope is there. Of course there are a lot of times when you can't see what hold you're going to and it's necessary to feel around, but I find that I (and others I've seen) often waste energy by failing to climb accurately. This is especially important with regards to footwork.

The idea of accuracy in climbing might sound a bit odd at first, but think about it. How many times have you fallen on a route because your foot wasn't exactly where it needed to be? How many times have your fingers peeled off of a hold because you failed to grab the sweet spot?

When you're lunging for a hold, don't just lunge blindly. Focus on exactly where your fingers need to be and make sure you get them there the first time. Lock your eyes on your target and make that right move on the first try.

Sure, sometimes you'll get lucky and can reposition your hands or feet, but other times you'll be dangling upside down on the end of your rope before you know what happened. Focus on accuracy and you'll notice that you can hang in there longer on those desperate redpoint and onsight attempts.

# 12. Assume Any New Partner Is an Idiot

I remember reading a forum post online by a guy who dropped the climber he was belaying. The belayer said that he warned the climber when he was at the halfway point of the rope, but the climber kept on climbing. As the belayer was lowering the climber, the belayer ran out of rope and the climber dropped to the ground.

Both parties are to blame here, and that made me think about how crazy it is that we as climbers often place our lives in the hands of strangers. Tennis players and online gamers certainly don't require that level of trust and mutual competency.

I figure the best thing to do when climbing for the first time with someone is to just assume they don't know anything.

Check and double-check everything. Check your harnesses and tie-in knots. Check that the leader has all the gear he or she will need. Go over procedures ("OK, so when I get to the top, I'm going to do X and then YOU are going to do Y") and commands ("When I say 'OFF!'...").

Do as much as you can before either of you starts climbing to ensure that everything will go as smoothly as possible.

# 13. A Basic First Aid Kit for Climbing

It's always a good idea to have a small first aid kit in your crag pack. Here's the stuff that you should have in a basic kit that is up to the task of treating most cuts, scrapes, pains, and blisters that you'll get when climbing:

**Tape** – You probably already have some sports tape in your climbing kit. If so, great. If not, you can wrap a small amount of sports tape or medical tape around a straw, pen, or stick.

**Moleskin** – This stuff is great for blisters, both in preventing them in the first place and covering them once they've formed.

**Band-Aids** – Protect those small cuts and help them heal.

**Antibacterial cream (e.g., Neosporin)** – This disinfectant cream will help the aforementioned small cuts not turn into festering wounds. It will also help the wound heal better and faster.

**Ibuprofen** – This stuff is anti-inflammatory and will reduce fever, pain, and swelling.

**Small scissors** – Useful for cutting moleskin or bandages to smaller sizes, among other things. I use a small Swiss Army knife that has scissors, a knife, tweezers, etc.

**Moist towelettes** – Use these to clean hands and wounds.

I have all of this stuff in a small plastic Ziploc bag. The kit is always kept in the lid pocket of my top-loading crag pack. I don't actually climb with this first aid kit unless I climb with my pack (which I try not to do as much as possible because I hate climbing with a pack), so I have it mostly for cragging days. For multi-pitch stuff where I'm not carrying the pack, I sometimes pare down the kit to just a few items that I can stick in a pocket.

If you don't have these items already and don't want to buy all of them individually, you can buy a small ready-made first aid kit for a few dollars at a grocery store, convenience store, or pharmacy.

# 14. Helping New Climbers Overcome Embarrassment

It's not uncommon for me to go climbing with people who are slightly embarrassed and self-conscious about their climbing abilities or, more specifically, their lack thereof. Maybe they're brand new to climbing and not very good, maybe they're a bit heavier set, or maybe they're scared. Whatever the reason, it can definitely hurt their enjoyment of the climbing experience. Here are some things you can do to make it a positive experience for them:

1. Put them on easy routes that they will succeed on. This will heighten their sense of accomplishment.

2. Don't comment about how easy a route is. The new climber might not think it's so easy.

3. Point out and compliment them on their successes. Even if the climber doesn't make it to the top of the route, you can still say, "Wow, you've got amazing footwork!" or, "You really nailed the bottom part."

4. Take them to a climbing area that isn't very crowded. The more people (especially unfamiliar people) that are around, the more uncomfortable the climber might be.

5. Don't show off. Yeah, you're probably able to climb the 5.6 that they struggled on, but you don't need to go campus your way up the 5.13 around the corner.

6. Invite other new climbers. Compared to you, the climber might not be very strong, but he won't feel so bad about his abilities if he sees someone else who is at his same level.

7. Encourage the new climbers to not get too caught up in a single climb. Stress that no one climb is all that important. Talk about how you just enjoy being outside and that success on a route is not the determining factor of whether you are happy (that is true, right?).

# 15. Getting (and Staying) Psyched

Every year I try to go to the Banff Mountain Film Festival, Reel Rock Film Tour, and whatever other mountain or adventure film showings I can find. One year of the Reel Rock Film Tour sticks out in my mind. We were shown six different short climbing films that covered sport climbing, bouldering, trad climbing, big wall climbing, and alpine climbing.

Although I enjoyed each film, I admit that I liked some of the films more than others. Watching Ueli Steck solo the north face of the Eiger in 2 hours 47 minutes inspired me much more than seeing V16 first ascents, for example (that's just me; your mileage may vary). The end result was that my buddy and I were unbelievably psyched as we drove home from the screenings. We each had a stronger resolve to train harder, climb harder, and climb more.

That wasn't the first time I'd felt that way. I swear before every winter that this winter will be the one where I build a home climbing wall or get a gym membership and train my brains out. Unfortunately, it never happens. So let's explore some ways to get psyched—that is, to get excited about climbing—along with some ways to make sure the psyche lasts longer than the short drive home.

## Getting psyched

1. Read climbing magazines. The great writing and photography are sure to inspire you.

2. Look on climbing websites at routes you want to do and areas you want to visit. Read trip reports about routes on your tick list.

3. Watch climbing videos. Nothing motivates me than seeing other people climb super hard.

4. Do the kinds of climbs that you enjoy. If you love long, moderate trad climbs, don't spend all your time bouldering.

## Staying psyched

1. Keep the psych alive! Whichever of the above methods works for you for getting psyched, keep doing it.

2. Climb with people who are as psyched as you are. Positive energy is infectious.

3. Climb with people who are better than you. Or continue watching better climbers climb. You'll be inspired to try harder.

4. Remember how good it feels to succeed and how fulfilling it is. Visualize that and remind yourself of it.

5. Climb a route every once in a while. What I mean by this is that it can be depressing to work on routes for ages and ages and never successfully redpoint anything. Make sure you do actually successfully get up something once in a while.

6. Recognize every success. Success in climbing doesn't always mean getting to the top of a route without falling. Sometimes it means linking a sequence for the first time. Sometimes it means going to a new climbing area. And sometimes it can just mean getting out of the house.

# 16. Remind the Newbies to Bring Water

I've noticed that whenever I take people climbing for their first time, they don't bring enough water. Sometimes they don't even bring any water, but usually they just don't bring enough. If you're climbing in a hot, dry, and/or humid place, you need to watch over your newbie friends. Make sure those beginners bring enough water. Then hopefully you won't have to share any of your own precious supply with anyone.

# 17. Breathe

"Breathe, dude! Breathe!" If I had a nickel for every time I've heard that...

I've been climbing for nearly two decades, and remembering to properly breathe when I climb a difficult route is still something that I have trouble with. I'm so caught up in just trying to hold on or make it to the next hold that I guess I forget about breathing. I think that part of me subconsciously feels that if I breathe, I will lose my body tension and peel right off. Unfortunately, it's kind of hard for your body to function at a high level without oxygen.

Before a hard climb, I usually ask my belayer to be watching me and to remind me to breathe. Hence the "Breathe, dude! Breathe!" Listen to your own breathing. Make it a point to breathe audibly. Get into a rhythm.

# General Climbing Tips

# 18. How to Read a Route in Six Steps

I think that one of the biggest advantages you can give yourself before getting on a route is looking at it and climbing it in your head. I've heard boulderers refer to this as "Buddha-ing" a route. The more you know about a route and what you can expect, the greater your chances of success. So here are six things you can do before you even start climbing that will help you climb to your full potential:

**1. Avoid the ground fall** – If you're climbing a sport route, how does the climbing look before the first bolt? Do you need to stick clip it? What holds will you clip that first bolt from? If you're trad climbing, where will you place your first and second pieces of gear that will keep you from hitting the ground?

**2. Rack accordingly (part 1)** – Look up at the climb. Look down at your gear. Look up at the climb again, maybe squinting this time. And then eye your gear again. I know some people who take a full set of cams (micro to offwidth) on every route they do. Now, friends, if you're looking up at a crack and can plainly see that it's a fingertip crack, you don't need to take that #4 offwidth piece. Does the crack lean or the pitch wander? If so, take extra long slings. If it's a sport route, make sure you've got enough draws for all of the bolts plus whatever you need for the anchors.

**3. Rack accordingly (part 2)** – Rack the pieces you know you'll be using up on the front loops of your harness so they're easy to find and grab.

**4. Find the crux** – Sometimes you can tell where the crux of a route will be just by eyeballing the route from the ground. Once you've identified it, you can pace yourself or conserve energy accordingly.

**5. Look for rests** – Are there any obvious rests that you can milk, especially before the crux?

**6. Plan for the worst** – If this is a route where you're pushing your limits, consider what you'll do if you don't make it to the top. Do you have a leaver carabiner or two handy? Will you have enough rope to lower down or rappel off?

# 19. Record Your Climbs

I was going through some of my stuff recently and found a climbing log that I kept for the first half of last year. Not only was it fun to look at those recorded climbs and remember them all (I wash shocked at how many I'd forgotten), but those notes will be useful for me if I ever repeat those routes in the future or if others ask me for beta.

When I take notes on a route, I record the climb name, area, route difficulty and length, quality, gear needed, date climbed, and any other beta or comments I've got. To record your climbs you can use an online database like Mountain Project, a spreadsheet, Google Maps, or any old notebook. If nothing else, record your climbs so that your kids will know how rad you were.

# 20. The Benefits of Climbing at Multiple Areas

I once read a great article by legendary climbing training guru Eric Hörst. In the article, Eric gave the challenge to climb at three new areas this season and said, "Climbing at many different areas is the very best investment in your future climbing ability."

I'd never thought of that up until that point, but it makes sense. There are a number of reasons why climbing at multiple areas is good for you. First, different rock types require different techniques. Climbing pocketed limestone is very different from climbing smooth granite, and both require different skills and approaches. Not only will this make you a better and more well-rounded climber, but you'll also gain confidence in your climbing ability. Once you climb at a lot of different areas, you'll think, "Well, I can climb here and here, so climbing there shouldn't be a problem." Either that or you'll get humbled by that old school trad 5.7+ and stop acting like such a hotshot. Either way, it's good to have other standards at which to compare your abilities. Your strengths and weaknesses are made more apparent, and you can work accordingly to improve areas in which you fall short.

There are plenty of other benefits to climbing at multiple areas. You stay psyched! I used to live literally four or five minutes from a canyon with more than 500 routes (I'd walk there when I didn't have a car), and this is where I did a lot of my early climbing. And even though this one canyon has both limestone and quartzite and everything from single pitch sport lines to multi-pitch trad lines, sometimes I just needed a change of scenery. It's always nice to get away from the home turf. Going to a new area can get you excited about climbing again if you're enthusiasm is waning.

Climbing at other areas also gets you more familiar with your gear and its placement. Placing cams in a splitter sandstone crack is very different from placing them in jagged quartzite scars. Some rock types take nuts more readily than others. Some areas have a lot of horizontal cracks while others have only hairline cracks. You get the idea.

And finally, climbing at other areas gives you a greater appreciation for climbing culture. You get to see how it all works at other areas: the types of bolts and anchors, the trails, the access issues, etc. You'll also meet a wider variety of people that can help you broaden your climbing horizons.

## 21. 10 Tips for Climbing in the Heat

Here are some ways to climb in the heat and still have an enjoyable time:

**1. Bring appropriate food** – Some food is just incredibly unappetizing when it's hot outside. I love peanut butter sandwiches, but it's almost impossible for me to choke them down when the mercury climbs.

**2. Wear the right clothes** – Wear shorts. Wear light-colored clothing. Wear loose-fitting clothing that breathes well.

**3. Bring sun protection** – This includes a hat, sunglasses, and sunscreen.

**4. Wear light-colored shoes** – If you've got multiple pairs of climbing shoes, consider wearing the pair that isn't entirely covered in black rubber or that isn't dark purple. The dark colors absorb the sun's heat and will make your feet feel like they're being seared with a blowtorch.

**5. Stay hydrated** – Bring tons of water, Gatorade, or whatever kind of drink you like.

**6. Have a reward in mind** – Promise yourself that you'll go get a nice refreshing Coke, Slurpee, snow cone, or ice cream as soon as you get off of the mountain. I promise you that nothing will ever have tasted so good.

**7. Climb in the shade** – Duh. You'll be able to find a shaded wall in most climbing areas.

**8. Climb at the right times** – Climb in the morning or evening, when it's cooler outside and when the wall you want to climb on is out of the sun.

**9. Climb near water** – To some this means deep water soloing. To others this could mean climbing in a narrow gorge or canyon with a stream at the bottom.

**10. Head for the hills** – If possible, climb at higher (cooler) elevations.

## 22. Some Thoughts on Climbing a Lot of Routes in a Day

Last year I was dealing with an injury and couldn't climb for a little while.

When I finally went climbing again, I ended up doing 15 single-pitch sport routes, none of which I'd done before, in a day. For me, that's a lot of routes. And man oh man did it feel good.

Sure, it can be fun to spend all day projecting a route at your limit, but it can be equally fun and gratifying to get a lot of mileage under your belt. Here are some tips to help you climb a bunch of routes in a day:

1. Bring food. It needs to be real food that can satisfy the hunger of a ravenous climber. On the day I climbed 15 routes, I brought Starbursts, some dried cranberries, and a granola bar. I didn't have anything else at home, so I didn't bring anything else. I got pretty hungry before I was ready to stop climbing, and I could have climbed even more routes if I'd brought along a nice pastrami on rye.

2. The main reason I didn't climb any more routes that day was that my arms were dead. Several of the harder routes we did were steep and pumpy, a style that is not my strong point. The plan was to do all of the climbs in a certain area by starting on the right-most route on each cliff and climbing each route to the left in turn. Unfortunately, this left a couple of the harder (and steeper) routes for the end, and my arms were just about dead by then. Do the harder routes early on while you've still got the juice.

3. Stay hydrated. If it's hot, bring frozen drinks (see the next tip). Warm water is gross.

4. Take temperature and sun position into consideration. The air temperature on my day of 15 routes wasn't too bad, but the sun was shining directly into our eyes for a while there. It was really annoying. If we'd planned better, we'd have been able to avoid that.

5. Take breaks if you need to. If you're going to climb for a full day, taking an afternoon siesta for an hour or two isn't that big of a deal if it means you'll climb better.

# 23. Freeze Some Gatorade for Hot Days

Get a couple of the small Gatorade (or Powerade or any other similar sports drink) bottles and stick them in the freezer before a trip. Bring them with you and leave them in the car to celebrate your triumphant and safe return, lug them to the base of a crag, or take a small one up a climb with you and drink it on top. By the time you get around to drinking it, it'll have thawed enough to make it drinkable, but there will still be some frozen chunks in there to keep it cold. It makes for a delightful and refreshing treat. You can almost feel the sugary energy coursing through your veins.

## 24. Are You Prepared for the Worst-Case Scenario?

Two of my good friends and climbing partners were involved in a climbing accident. They were bolting a new multi-pitch sport route on lead when falling rocks hit the leader. I would have been there with them but was taking another friend and his visiting brother climbing for the day.

The details of what exactly happened are fuzzy, but the leader was hit in the head and took a big fall. He was wearing a helmet, but it was crushed and ripped off of his head (always wear a helmet!). The belayer lowered him to a ledge and called 911. An hour later, the injured climber was flown to the hospital. In the end, he had a concussion, some cracked vertebrae, and a broken hand, but it could have been much worse.

Both of these climbers are extremely experienced, each with decades of climbing experience.

Accidents really can happen to anyone at any time. Luckily, the belayer in the case mentioned above had his cell phone with him and could call for help. But what if he hadn't brought it? What if he didn't get cell phone reception? What if they were climbing in the backcountry and were several hours (or even days) away from help? What would you do if your partner got hurt? Do you know how to treat injuries? Do you know how to lower an injured climber?

Ask yourself these questions when you're climbing and see what the answers are. If you have no idea what you'd do in a sticky situation, what do you have to do to learn? Climbing is a serious sport, especially if you're off the beaten path. Be safe out there and have a contingency plan for the worst-case scenario.

## 25. How to Get Back to Steep Rock After a Fall

You're on a very steep route and take a fall when you're halfway between bolts. Now you're dangling there in the air, not touching any rock. How do you get back to the rock? Well, you could use ascenders or prusiks to climb the rope back to your highpoint, but no one wants to take ascenders on a sport route. Thankfully, there is a simple way of getting back to the rock that is pretty easy to do unless you've got a looong way to go to get back to the rock, in which case it will get pretty tiring.

So let's say you've fallen and can't get back to the cliff. You're just hanging there. Grab the rope above you with both hands, do a quick pull-up, and let go of the rope when you're at the top of the pull-up. For a second, there will be slack in the rope, and your ever-attentive belayer can take in that slack. Voila! You're up a few inches or a foot (8 or 30 centimeters), depending on how hard you pull up and how fast your belayer is. Figure 2 illustrates the technique.

Like I said, it would get really tiring to go up 30 feet using this method (and it would hurt your hands after a while), but it's a good trick to know about and use when the rock is within striking distance.

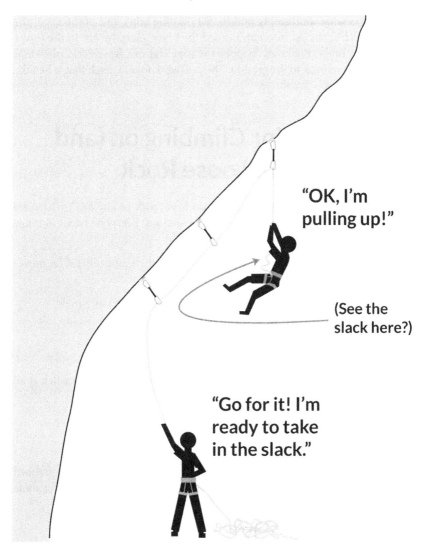

Figure 2. Getting back to steep rock after a fall (Tip #25)

# 26. So You Pulled the Rope but Forgot to Take the Knot Out

This has happened to me exactly one time. I led a sport route, lowered off, and untied. My climbing partner pulled the rope but realized too late that I hadn't fully untied the 8 left by my mostly untied figure eight tie-in knot. The rope wouldn't slide through the anchors at the top, and we couldn't retrieve it. Rookie mistake, right?

So this is what we did: My buddy tied into the other end of the rope (the end not stuck at the anchors) and re-led the route. Once he got to the top of the pitch, he undid the knot, dropped the rope end that was previously stuck, and was lowered back to the ground. This will work for any pitch that is half the length of your rope or shorter.

# 27. 23 Tips for Climbing on (and Dealing With) Loose Rock

Not every climb is squeaky clean with no loose rock of any kind. There are incredibly classic routes that still have loose sections. Everyone needs to know how to deal with bad rock. Here are 23 ways:

1. Be careful and alert when pulling your ropes when rappelling. The movement of a rope that's being pulled can dislodge loose rocks.

2. Look for other ways around loose blocks and sections of loose rock.

3. Wear a helmet!

4. Make sure your partner has a helmet too.

5. Test your holds. Gingerly put some weight on them to see if they flex at all before committing your weight to the hold.

6. Pull down on the handholds, not out.

7. Keep as much weight over your feet as possible.

8. Look for holds with chalk on them. This means that someone has grabbed the hold before, which means it has probably held someone's weight at some point. Don't forget to test even these holds.

9. Visually inspect holds. Are there fracture lines around the hold?

10. Rockfall often occurs in the morning as the sun warms the rock/ice/snow.

Be aware of this.

11. Don't climb below other parties.

12. Try not to rappel above other parties.

13. Sometimes it's better not to place gear behind hollow flakes or other kinds of suspect rock, even if that means a longer runout. It can be nice to have that psychological protection, but if you do fall, there's a chance that the loose flake or block could come down with you and kill you, kill your belayer, or cut your rope.

14. Yell "ROCK!" as loud as you can if you do dislodge something, and pray that it doesn't hit anyone.

15. Strategically place your gear and use slings to keep your rope away from rubbing against loose sections of rock.

16. Spend as little time as possible at the base of routes. This cuts down on the amount of time you spend in the potential line of fire.

17. If possible, belay off to the side of a leader instead of directly below her.

18. When you're belaying, take shelter under a roof or bulge if there is one.

19. Know that there will be more loose rock in the spring and early summer than in late summer, both because of the freeze-thaw cycles and because previous parties haven't yet had the chance to knock the loose stuff off.

22. Know that rain can also cause rockfall.

23. Animals like mountain goats can knock rocks down onto you. Keep your eyes peeled for the animals and avoid climbing directly below them.

# 28. 9 Times When It's NOT OK to Fall

Remember how the old trad climbers from back in the day had the whole "the leader must not fall" mindset? I think that falling can be healthy. If you're not willing to push yourself and fall, you're not going to get better as a climber. There's a big asterisk next to that statement, however. Sometimes you just don't fall. Here are some of those times:

**1. Before you get to the first bolt or put your first piece in** – This one's obvious. If you fall before your rope is clipped into something, there's nothing there to arrest your fall. You'll hit the ground and it'll hurt. Going along with this, don't fall any time there's ground fall potential. Bad idea.

**2. When the rock is bad** – Sometimes the rock your gear is in just isn't very good. If the crack you've got that cam in is shattered, loose, and crumbly, you shouldn't tempt fate by falling on it.

**3. When the gear placements are marginal** – Don't fall on bad gear. Duh.

**4. When your leg is in front of the rope** – You'll get flipped upside down and could bonk your head. Remember tip #2?

**5. When you're looking at a biiiiig fall** – Sometimes you can take a big fall and come out unscathed, but the longer your air time, the bigger your chance of getting injured.

**6. When you'll hit something if you fall** – Don't fall when you're above a ledge; you'll break your ankles on the thing. Don't fall on a traverse from a dihedral out onto a face, because you'll pendulum into the corner. You get the idea.

**7. When the rope is in between your teeth** – You know how a lot of people, when they're clipping the rope into protection, hold the rope in their mouths for a bit while they're grabbing more slack? Can you imagine how horrible it would be to fall with the rope in your mouth? I remember reading a story in *Climbing* magazine several years ago that talked about that very thing. Most of the guy's teeth got ripped out. Yikes.

**8. When there are loose blocks around** – You don't want to fall and knock a bunch of loose rocks and blocks onto your belayer.

**9. While you're placing gear** – Because you'll probably end up dropping it.

# 29. 5 Tips for Getting Over Your Climbing Plateau

One of the greatest parts about climbing is that there's always room for improvement. We can always track our progress and keep getting better. But a lot of climbers eventually get to a point where they feel like they've stopped progressing. This can happen after a couple months of climbing or after 10 years of climbing. While I think a lot of us would agree that grades in and of themselves don't matter all that much, the harder we are able to climb, the more climbs are available to us, so constantly increasing in climbing ability is generally desirable. There are a bunch of different things you can do to get over this plateau:

1. Be realistic about your goals, abilities, and time frame – I once heard some-

one say that he was frustrated that he couldn't climb V3s after two months of climbing. Come on! Some people are NEVER able to climb a V3 boulder problem, and the same can be said for essentially every grade in climbing. Climbing is hard work, and it's a lifetime pursuit for a lot of people. Realize that these things do take time. Just because you went from V0 to V2 in a week, that doesn't mean you'll be able to go from V2 to V4 in a week.

2. Start projecting – I'm not a patient person, and that definitely carries over into climbing. I've never had much interest in projecting routes; I'm too impatient, and it frustrates me to work the same moves over and over. But the simple fact of the matter is that to go to the next level in your climbing, you're going to have to work routes multiple times. Find a project that inspires you and get after it. If you're stuck at mid-5.11 and are depressed because you can't string more than two moves together on your first attempt of a 5.12a, it's OK. Continue working on the route. If you work on it long enough, you'll climb the thing. If there's any route you can almost climb, you'll eventually be able to climb it if you stick with it.

3. Focus on your technique – Good technique will make any climb easier, whether it be 5.8 or 5.13. But for most people, it's when you get into the 5.10 range that proper technique really starts making life a lot easier. What do I mean by "good technique"? Be comfortable with things like drop knees, flagging, stepping through, back stepping, rotating your hips, knee bars, keeping your arms straight, etc. Go dig out one of those "how-to" climbing books you got when you first started climbing and see what basics you're missing out on.

4. Focus on your weaknesses – If you can't for the life of you hold on to sloping holds, go out and climb routes with a bunch of slopers on them, even if that means climbing routes that may otherwise be well below your ability. You could also strengthen your weaknesses by getting a hangboard or gym membership and focusing on the grips or holds you want to get better at.

5. Quantity – I found this great blurb on the *Rock and Ice* website a while back:

"Dani Andrada, one of the best climbers in the world, was rumored to have redpointed 50 5.13b's before he even considered getting on a 5.13c. While those grades are admittedly elite, the lesson still applies: Take the time needed to master the easier grades before moving on. Did you redpoint 50 5.11d's before even trying a 5.12a?"

In other words, have you put in the necessary work at a lower grade to make climbing at a higher grade realistic?

# Sport Climbing Tips

# 30. Making a Stiffy, the Sport Climber's Secret Weapon

Figure 3. The stiff quickdraw or "stiffy" (Tip #30)

This thing is freaking awesome. It's a quickdraw with clear plastic tubing over the webbing part. The tubing is long enough that it pushes up significantly on both carabiners, keeping them in place. This creates a stiff quickdraw, or as I like to call it, a stiffy. Mine is shown in Figure 3.

Another method that I've heard of other climbers using but never done myself is to use duct tape to tape some coat hanger wire to the webbing to make it stiff.

Why is this so great? It lets you clip bolts and other fixed gear (I've used it to clip fixed pitons on aid routes) that are just out of reach. It's like a mini stick clip. I've used it dozens of times on sport routes to clip a just-barely-out-of-reach bolt before a cruxy move. The diameter and length of your tubing will vary according to the size of your draws. I just took my draw with me when I went into the home improvement store and tried sticking the webbing into the tubing until I got a good fit. The tubing will be in the plumbing department and is very cheap.

Try it. You'll love it. If you find yourself using it often, make a couple more.

# 31. How to Clean a Sport Route

This is the quintessential beginner question. How do you get off of a sport climb without leaving any of your gear behind? Great question! There are many ways to do it, but I feel like the method below is the safest and most foolproof option. When you get to the top of a sport route, clip straight into the anchors. The best and safest way to do this is to have two shoulder-length (24-inch/30-centimeter) slings girth-hitched to your harness's belay loop. I'd say get the skinniest ones you can find so they don't bulk up your harness too much. Each sling should have a carabiner on it, ideally a locking carabiner. While you're climbing, the slings should be clipped off to your back gear loops on either side so that they're not in the way. You can use quickdraws if you don't have slings and carabiners, but slings with locking carabiners are easier and safer.

When you get to the anchors, unclip the carabiners from your harness and clip one carabiner (with its attached sling) to each bolt of the anchor. Pull up some slack in the rope (like you're clipping into a quickdraw on lead, but you'll want a bit more slack than that) and tie a figure eight on a bight or a clove hitch. With another carabiner (again, preferably locking), clip the knot into your belay loop.

The rope should now run from your belayer, through all of the quickdraws on the route (including a couple of draws clipped into the anchors if you feel that you need to do that), to the knot that is clipped to your harness. There should be a loop of rope hanging down between the clipped-off knot on your belay loop and the original tie-in point of your harness. Make sure you're still on belay so that if something crazy happens (i.e., the anchors somehow give way) and you fall, your belayer will still catch you. Now untie your original tie-in point, thread the rope through the anchors (usually rings or chains of some sort; you want to thread it through the bottom-most rings or chain links) and tie the rope back to your harness like you normally would.

Now unclip the locking carabiner that is attached to the loop of rope on your belay loop and drop the loop of rope. Have your belayer take in the slack and confirm that you are indeed still on belay. Unclip your carabiners (the ones that are attached to your slings) from the anchors. Your weight will now be held by your belayer. The rope will be running from your belayer up through the anchors and then back to you (you're tied into the end). Have your belayer lower you down, and you're good to go. Remove your draws (or gear if it's a trad route) on your way down.

You may want to rappel instead of be lowered. Rappelling is actually better for the anchors because it causes less wear on the chains or rings of the anchor; the weighted rope running through the anchors causes them to wear out faster. If you want to rappel, follow the above steps up to the point where you've pulled up some rope and clipped it into your harness. You should have already clipped in to the anchors with your carabiners and slings. Once you've pulled up the rope and clipped it to your harness, untie the end of rope from your harness and thread it through the anchors. Tie a knot in that end of the rope and pull the rope through until you need to unclip the rope from your harness. Unclip (the reason you want to clip the rope to your harness is that you don't want to drop the rope while you're threading it through the anchors; that would be bad!) and continue to pull the rope through until the middle of the rope (you did mark the middle, didn't you?) is right at the anchors. Thread the rope through your rappel device, attach the rappel device to your harness with a locking carabiner, and take in all slack in the rope above the rappel device until your weight is being held by the rappel device instead of the slings attached to the anchors. Unclip those slings, store them safely out of the way by clipping them to your harness, and rappel, cleaning your quickdraws (or protection if it's a trad route) as you go.

Ta da! You're back on the ground.

## 32. Put the Rope Over Your Shoulder While You're Getting to the First Bolt

Before you get to the first bolt (or before you put your first piece of protection in on a trad route), put the rope over your shoulder. The rope will go from the tie-in points on your harness up and over one of your shoulders, then over your back and down to your belayer. This way, the rope is out of the way of your feet and easier (and faster) to grab when you clip in. Just make sure you clip it in the right way so that your end of the rope goes up through the bottom carabiner it's clipped into and not down.

## 33. Get Some Long Quickdraws

You know how sometimes you just want to buy gear because you like new gear? Of course you do. We're climbers, and coveting gear is part of the game. I was bored one day and decided to go to the local climbing shop and spend the extra $10 I had on whatever tickled my fancy. A long (12-inch/30-centimeter) quickdraw caught my attention. Most of my draws are short little guys except for one longer (9-inch/23-centimeter) draw that I bootied a while back and really like. I felt that my quickdraw rack could use a little more diversity, so I bought the thing.

I have to admit that this was probably one of my better impromptu gear purchases. It's not uncommon to feel rope drag on sport climbs, but for some reason most of us never use long slings like we do when trad climbing. Having one (or a few) of these long draws in your quickdraw quiver is perfect for that "why-on-earth-did-they-put-the-bolt-way-over-there?!" clip. I wouldn't recommend getting a dozen of these things, but my two longer draws have definitely been put to good use. I also find myself taking these draws with me on trad climbs.

# 34. How to Clean Overhanging or Traversing Sport Routes

Severely overhanging or traversing routes create a problem when you try to clean them. If you were just lowered straight down, you wouldn't be able to reach the draws to clean them. The solution? Trolleying. It's when you clip one end of a quickdraw to your belay loop and the other to the rope. As you get lowered down, you slide along the rope, as shown in Figure 4.

Because of all the tension on the rope, it might be hard to unclip the rope from the draws. If that happens, you can unclip your harness's trolleying quickdraw from the rope and clip it directly onto the bolt. This unweights the rope, making it possible for you to remove the quickdraw that was previously under too much tension. Then unclip the bolt end of the harness quickdraw and reattach it to the rope. Be prepared for some wrangling followed by a little swing.

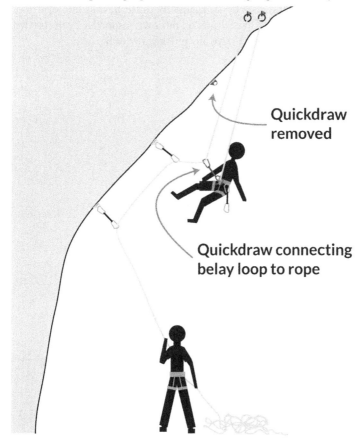

*Figure 4. A climber "trolleying" in on an overhanging sport climb (Tip #34)*

# 35. How Many Quickdraws Do You Need?

For years I had 12 quickdraws, and this was almost always sufficient, but I would say that 14 is the magic number.

That said, there are thousands of routes across the country (and around the world) that you could climb with 8 draws, or even 6. But 14 draws will let you climb any 12-bolt route and still have two draws left for the anchors. Very rarely will you need more than that. And if you do need more than that, you can use slings or borrow draws from friends.

Sometimes you'll need more draws on a multi-pitch sport route. If that's the case, you can always combine quickdraw racks with your partner.

Some areas have really short walls. If your local crag is only 30 feet (10 meters) tall, you're not going to need a ton of draws.

I currently have 26 draws. Why so many? Because having lots of draws allows me and a buddy to both have draws on our own respective projects (two separate routes), even if he doesn't have any quickdraws of his own.

# Trad Climbing Tips

# 36. What's the Best Way to Start Trad Climbing?

You think you're hardcore, and everyone else thinks so too. You climb V10000 boulder problems and warm up on 5.13s with two lucky ladies dangling from your rippling back muscles. Life is good. But you have a dirty little secret. You're afraid, but not of any 5.14 gut-wrenching mono ladder. No. You're afraid of the 5.8 fist crack at your local chossbucket crag. You don't trad climb under the pretenses of it being "too easy," and you just wanting to "focus on the movement, brah."

The truth, however, is that the idea of trusting your life to Bazooka gum-sized pieces of aluminum shoved into weaknesses (weaknesses!) in the rock gives you the heebie-jeebies. As you pass the 5.8 crack on your way to your double-dyno sick proj, you silently curse the climbing gods. "How?!" you ask in anger. "How do I become a trad climber??" In that moment, the clouds part, the sun shines through, and angels sing. Your prayers are about to be answered.

(Note: You don't have to sport climb before you trad climb, but that seems to be the route that most people take. My first lead ever was a trad pitch in Yosemite. Regardless, I'm assuming here that you already understand the fundamentals of leading.)

The single best thing you can do to become a trad climber is apprentice yourself to a Jedi trad master. Be Anakin to his Obi-Wan. Have him (or her) lead all of the trad climbs, and you follow all of the pitches (multi-pitch) or toprope the route (single pitch). You remove all the gear that the leader placed. Cleaning gear lets you see what fits where and how it fits there. Do this for a while. Follow and clean as many pitches as you can. As you're doing this, pay close attention to what pieces fit in what size cracks. For me, for example, a tight hand crack takes a red (#1) Camalot, a perfect hand crack takes a gold (#2), and so on.

While you've got Obi-Wan around, grab his/her gear and practice placing his/her cams and nuts in the cracks at ground-level. This gives you firsthand experience with placing gear without any I'm-gonna-die-if-I-fall-here moments. Try pulling on the gear, then clip in to a long sling. Put your foot in the sling and bounce around a lot to become confident that those little aluminum doohickeys really can save your butt.

Somewhere in here I should mention that it's not a bad idea to get a book that describes how to place cams and nuts. (I hate hexes, so I won't talk about them.) Study it, live it, breathe it. No, books aren't substitutes for first-hand instruction, but it never hurts to responsibly know too much.

Now go find a super easy trad line, one that you probably wouldn't ever fall on, and practice placing gear on toprope. Rig up the climb just like you would any other toprope, but throw cams and nuts on your harness and practice placing them as you go up. Climb the route a bunch of times. Get the gear wired. You can also try tying into a rope and pretend you're on lead. Practice placing the gear and clipping the mock lead rope into it. You could also kick it up a notch and try leading for real on a lead line while simultaneously being backup belayed on toprope. Yeah, you'd need two belayers for this, but it might help with your confidence if you're still nervous.

If you want to gain even more confidence, take little falls onto your gear. Start out by just weighting the pieces, and then take a little fall. Once you realize that you're still alive, you'll be all sorts of brave.

By this point, you should know how to place gear. You should know when a cam is tipped out and when it's overcammed. You should know what makes a good nut placement. You should know that whatever piece you place (in good rock) will hold you and every overweight person you know. To me, that is the single most important thing to know. Your gear will hold if you place it correctly and the rock is good.

Now you're ready for the real deal. Lead that route that you've toproped to death. You'll dominate it. Remember that for many, trad climbing is a very mental game. Just keep breathing and keep telling yourself that you'll be fine if you do fall (which you shouldn't on this route, right?). And guess what. Congratulations! You're a trad climber now!

The order described here isn't sacred. You can practice placing gear on toprope, for example, before you follow an old coot up a bunch of routes. Do what works for you. Just don't die. Know what you're doing before you do it, and climb with people who know what they're doing. When you're ready, there's that 5.8 chossbucket fist crack to take down.

# 37. Should You Rack Trad Gear on a Sling or on Your Harness?

I got a little bit ahead of myself when I first started climbing. I bought my cams before I had really done any trad climbing. I also bought a gear sling with those cams. On my very first lead, I had a brand new set of cams dangling from a brand new adjustable gear sling. As soon as I started climbing, I thought, "Hmmm... This sucks..." The gear kept shifting in front of me, obstructing my view of my feet. Since I was on a slab, this was problematic. I managed to finish the climb, but being unable to see my feet certainly didn't help my beginner's nerves. (I have since learned that the gear sling was way too long; I should have shortened it up.)

For my second trad climb, I ditched the gear sling and racked the gear on my harness's gear loops instead. The experience was a lot better. Everything stayed put, and I had full view of my feet. I could focus on being scared because leading was terrifying instead of being scared because I couldn't see my feet.

Gear slings can be useful when you're climbing offwidths or chimneys and need to be able to rack more gear on one side of your body. They can also be helpful on multi-pitch climbs because they make it quick and easy to transfer gear between partners when switching leads—just hand over the sling and you're good to go.

Overall, though, I prefer racking gear on my harness to racking it on a gear sling.

# 38. How to Rack Gear on Your Harness

There are many different ways to rack gear on your harness. Figure 5 shows how I do it, and this is how I've seen a lot of other climbers do it. Note that I'm right-handed. You might want to flip things around if you're a lefty. I've put a number by each of the four gear loops in the illustration, and I explain below what I rack on each gear loop.

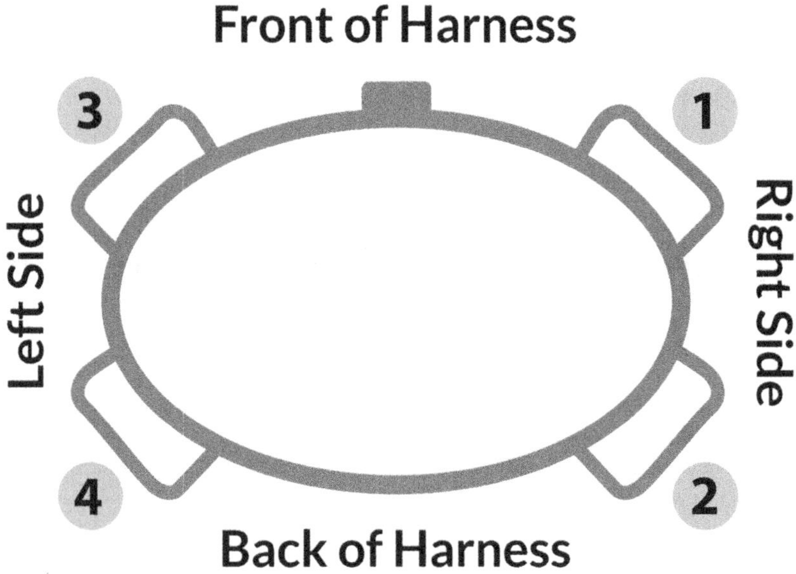

*Figure 5. How to rack gear on a harness (Tip #38)*

**Gear loop 1** – Set of nuts, small cams to wide fingers
**Gear loop 2** – The bigger cams
**Gear loop 3** – Quickdraws and trad draws
**Gear loop 4** – Belay device, cordalette, extra carabiners (regular and locking). Water bottles and approach shoes get clipped to this loop for multi-pitch routes.

This is my standard setup for trad climbing, and I use it on 95% of the trad climbs I do, whether they're single- or multi-pitch (though I don't take things like the cordalette or extra carabiners on single-pitch routes). I usually take a set of nuts and a set of cams with me up just about every route unless I can look at the route and see that I obviously won't need a size of gear. On routes where I bring doubles of certain sizes, I shift the cams around accordingly so that there's an even amount of weight on the front and back loops of the right side.

The important thing is to rack your gear in a way that works well for you and stick with it. After you've been climbing and place gear long enough, you'll know exactly where on your harness you need to reach for the right piece of gear.

## 39. Use Color-Coded Carabiners

I absolutely love having color-coded carabiners on my cams. I put a green carabiner on the sling of my green cam, a red carabiner on the sling of my red cam, and so on. This is helpful in two situations:

1. When you're pumped and you need to pick and grab your piece fast. Instead of having to grab a handful of cams on your harness and bring them up so you can see what color/size they are, you can easily just grab the colored carabiner that you need. For example, let's say I'm climbing a thin hand crack. I know that's a red (#1) Camalot, and I easily find and grab the cam by identifying the red carabiner.

2. When you've got a ton of gear on you (think aid climbing) and it's hard to find anything specific in the mass of webbing and aluminum.

A few different companies make color-coded carabiners. Get the sizes, styles, and colors you like best.

## 40. The Sub-$600 Beginner Trad Rack

"What trad gear should I get?" That question might get asked more than any other on climbing forums, and this is my very opinionated answer. The brands on everything here are pretty flexible; that is, I don't think it matters a whole lot what brand of carabiners or nuts you buy. Anything by any of the large gear companies (Black Diamond, Metolius, DMM, and Wild Country) will be high-quality and last for years. I'm partial to Black Diamond gear, so that's what I recommend most often. The items listed below are the perfect beginner trad rack and will set you back about $600.

**Black Diamond Camalots .5–3** – As of writing this, you can get a set of these five cams for around $315. Yes, there are cheaper cams out there, but none are better than Camalots, in my opinion. Buy the right thing the first time. These five sizes are good from finger-sized to fist-sized cracks.

**Set of nuts #4–#13** – Sizes 1–3 are very small and not super useful if you're just starting out. Black Diamond sells a 4–13 Stopper set that you can get for around $90. Other manufacturers offer similar deals. I've got a couple of these nuts by other companies mixed in with my Stoppers, and they're all essentially the same thing. If Stoppers don't appeal to you, buy the equivalent set of whatever brand does.

**6 24-inch (60-centimeter) slings** – You can either triple these into a trad draw (see tip #41) or wear them over your shoulder. These will cost you $30 at about $5 each. You can spend more and get the super sexy skinny ones. I think they're worth it if you've got the money. I do not recommend getting any made out of 1-inch (25-milimeter) webbing. It's just too fat. You could tie your own slings and save some money (I did that for several years), but sewn runners are definitely preferable.

**20 carabiners** – The classic offset D-shaped carabiner is the best and most common overall carabiner. You're going to want twelve of these for the slings (two on each sling), one for each of your cams, and two for the set of nuts (the small nuts on one carabiner and the larger ones on the other). That's 19 total. We'll bump it up to 20 because you can never have too many carabiners. At roughly $6 each, 20 of these puppies will set you back $120.

**Nut tool** – Get a nut tool with a carabiner built in. It'll cost around $15.

All of that adds up to roughly $570. Sweet! Buy your gear used and it'll be even less.

Figure 6 shows what all of that gear looks like.

# 41. Making a Trad Draw

Medium-length (24-inch/60-centimeter) slings are an essential part of any climber's kit. They're often carried over the shoulder (that is, across your chest like a bandolier or beauty queen sash), but sometimes these can be awkward to remove mid-climb. Enter the trad draw. The trad draw is a way to shorten these 24-inch slings so they can easily be carried on a harness. Figure 7 shows the process of making one.

To extend the slings, remove the draw from your harness or gear sling like you would a normal quickdraw. With your fingers (mainly your thumb and

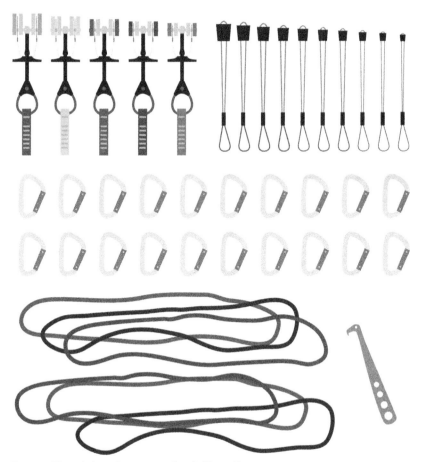

*Figure 6. The sub-$600 beginner trad rack (Tip #40)*

pointer finger, with the others assisting) remove any two of the three loops of webbing that go through the top carabiner. This might take some practice, but it's really easy once you've got the hang of it. After you've unclipped these two, you might need to shake the loops a bit to get the sling to fully extend.

## 42. The Better Way to Rack Your Nuts

Please, no jokes about racking your nuts.

For a long time I carried a set of nuts on one D-shaped carabiner. I remember a couple times in particular when I was fumbling around and trying to get a nut off the racking carabiner but the wire of the nut got snagged on the

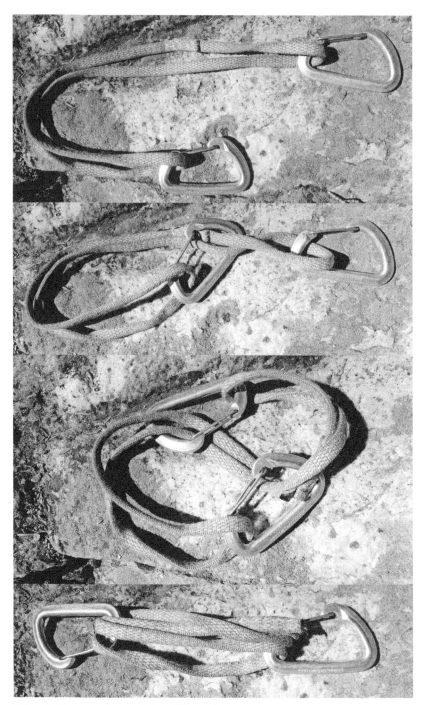

*Figure 7. How to make a trad draw (Tip #41)*

carabiner's notch. Not fun. There are three things you can do to alleviate this problem and make accessing your nuts easier:

**1. Get two separate carabiners** – Have one carabiner hold the bigger nuts and one carabiner hold the smaller nuts. I've found that with less weight on each carabiner and with fewer wires to mess with, it's easier to find, slot, and remove the nut I'm looking for.

**2. Get notchless (keylock) carabiners** – It's so nice for the nuts to be able to slide easily off the carabiner without having to worry about that stupid notch getting in the way

**3. Get oval carabiners** – Why? Because the basket on these (the bottom of the carabiner that the nuts hang from) is larger, and the wires don't get all jumbled up and intertwined. This might not be a huge problem, but it's a minor one that is easily remedied. Keeping this and the second tip in mind, what you're ideally looking for are two notchless oval carabiners to rack your nuts on.

# 43. Things to Consider When Buying Cams

Here we'll cover just about everything you need to know about cams, starting with the most basic things.

Cams have three or four lobes (the quarter-circle-shaped parts of a cam that come into contact with the rock). The lobes are connected to an axle (the part that the lobes rotate from), and the axle is connected to a longer stem. On the stem is what is referred to as a trigger. To insert a cam into a crack, you pull the trigger back with a finger or two while your thumb or the heel of your palm is holding the bottom of the stem. This retracts (pulls back) the lobes. The cam is then inserted into a crack (which is more or less parallel-sided), and the trigger is released. The cam lobes spring outward until they come in contact with the rock. The rope is then clipped into the sling that's attached to the stem.

Cams are a marvel of modern engineering. They do their job so well and make our job of climbing so much less dangerous and stressful. Cracks that used to be feared because they wouldn't accept passive protection or pitons are now easy pickings with cams.

Here are some things to consider when buying cams:

## Three lobes vs. Four lobes

Cams usually have either three of four lobes. Units with three lobes are for smaller cracks, usually about 1 inch (25 millimeters) or less in width. Four lobes are standard for larger-sized units. Three-lobed cams are nice because their head width is narrower than the comparably sized four-lobed cam, so they can fit in shallower cracks.

## Normal sling vs. Doubled sling

All cams have slings on them, but some have a sling that is doubled up. When doubled, the sling is one length. When one of the loops of the sling is unclipped from the carabiner, the other loop can be pulled, and the result is that the whole sling is extended to twice that original length. This is a very useful feature to have because it means that you don't have to carry quite as many additional slings with you. You'll still probably have to carry some slings, however, because even when the slings on the cams are extended, they're not super long.

## Single stem vs. Double stem

Cams have either one or two stems. On a single-stemmed cam, two of the four lobes are on one side of the stem and two are on the other. A double-stemmed cam has a U-shaped stem usually made from a cable of a smaller diameter. The cable is bent into the U shape, and the four lobes are sandwiched between the two tips of the U. Single-stemmed cams are easier to work with, in my opinion. I've had the cable stems of smaller double-stemmed cams get in the way of the good placement before.

It doesn't matter all that much which brand of cam you choose; it's mostly just a personal preference. Any cam from the major manufacturers is going to be bomber. Try as many different kinds as possible by using your partners' racks before buying a set of your own.

## Rigid stem vs. Flexible stem

The stem of nearly all cams these days is made from thick steel cable. The main exception, the Forged Friend by Wild Country, has a rigid stem that is essentially a little I-beam. This cam hasn't been produced for several years now, but there are still a lot of these cams out in the wild. If you're considering buying used cams, they're something you should be aware of.

Rigid-stemmed cams last forever. They're super burly and rugged. They are also very lightweight. With the smaller sizes, however, the rigid stem can get in the way of placing the unit optimally. In addition, placing a rigid cam in a shallow horizontal crack can possibly break the stem (though I've never heard of this actually happening) through leverage. This potential drawback can easily be fixed by using a Gunks tie-off on the cam. This consists of a loop of cord tied through a hole near the head of the cam. When placing the cam in a horizontal crack, you clip into this loop instead of the loop at the base of the stem.

Some "flexible" stems are more flexible than others. When place in vertical crack, the stems of some cams may move well side-to-side but flex very little up and down. Other cams have very flexible stems that will move in any direction.

This is especially useful in aid climbing where gear placements can get tricky, though the more flexible a stem is, the harder it can be to remove the cam. Flexible-stemmed cams can also absorb some of the routine movement of the rope and sling as you climb above the cam, thereby minimizing the amount of motion transferred to the cam lobes themselves. This motion to the cam lobes can cause them to move or "walk" into less than optimal places in the crack after they have been placed. A longer sling will solve this problem even with rigid-stemmed cams.

## Single axle vs. Double axle

Apart from a couple exceptions (namely the Metolius Supercam and Omega Pacific Link Cam), double-axle cams (like the Black Diamond Camalot and the similar cams it has inspired) have a greater expansion range, meaning that you can take fewer pieces to cover the same range, and a single piece will be able to fit a wider variety of crack sizes. Double-axle cams generally tend to be heavier, though lighter versions of these cams are being introduced. For general-purpose cams, I think that double-axle cams are hard to beat, and I wouldn't buy traditional single-axle cams unless I got a really great deal on them.

## Head width

As stated above, cams with three lobes generally and historically have had narrower head widths than cams with four lobes (though this is certainly not always the case). The reason a narrow head width is desirable in smaller units is that a narrow unit can fit in more places. With bigger units, however, it's less of an issue. Indeed, with offwidth-sized pieces, a wider head width is better because it is more stable and makes the cam less prone to motion and walking (think of it in terms of legs on a chair; it's easier to tip over a chair that has legs that are closer together).

## Cam stops

Cam stops are machined parts of the lobes or pins inserted into the lobes of a cam that prevent cam lobes from opening "upward" or "umbrella-ing." This is in issue if a cam walks back into a spot in the crack where the width is wider than optimal. In a worst-case scenario, the cam could collapse when fallen on, and the piece would pull out of the crack. Cam stops mitigate this concern. Some cams have full-strength cam stops, meaning that the cam could even be placed passively like a nut. Again, while I have rarely run into a situation where I've had to place cams passively, it's nice to have the option. Most cams these days do have integrated cam stops.

## Weight

The less your gear weighs, the better. A few grams here and there might not seem like a big deal, but they add up to a significant amount when taken in aggregate. Compare the weights of various models when shopping for cams, and take those weights into consideration when making your decision of which cams to purchase.

### Clip-in thumb loop

All cams have a sling of some sort attached to them, but take a look at how and where the sling is attached to the stem of the cam. On some cams, the sling is sewn to a large thumb loop. This is a desirable feature because when aid climbing, you can clip your aiders directly to this loop to gain a few extra inches of height.

## 44. Using Nuts as Slings

Some friends and I once climbed at cliff we didn't know much about. It was hard to tell exactly how tall the cliff was. I figured it was about 100 feet (30 meters) tall, but it turned out to be closer to 200 feet (60 meters). I only brought up a few slings with me for the lead and ran out of them about halfway up the wall. I still needed something to use to mitigate rope drag, so out came the nuts. To turn a nut into a makeshift sling, all you have to do is slide the nut itself down the cable and clip a carabiner to both ends. I try not to make a habit of this and it should be considered a last resort because the nuts I use (Black Diamond Stoppers) are only rated to 10 kN, while slings are rated to 22 kN. If you do use this trick, use the largest sizes of nuts first. They're the ones that are strongest. Using a nut as a sling is also not ideal because nuts are stiffer slings and could facilitate walking of active protection. But depending on the situation, it may be better than nothing.

## 45. Get Matching Slings in Different Sizes

One good thing about climbing with a lot of different people is that you can see how they do things, and you pick up all sorts of tips and tricks this way. One guy I climbed with a couple times had color-coded slings. All of his 24-inch (60-centimeter) slings were one color, all of his 48-inch (120-centimeter) slings another color, and so on. That way, when you've got a wad of nylon slung around your shoulders, you'll know what you're grabbing. If you don't normally carry 48-inch slings (or if you don't carry them around your shoulder) then this isn't a huge issue, though the coloring can still be helpful when all of your gear is mixed together in the giant plastic bin you store it in.

It's worth mentioning that color isn't the only differentiating factor you have to work with. Your different sling lengths can also be of different thicknesses or materials, and you'll still achieve the same effect of knowing at a glance the size of a given sling.

*Figure 8. Shortening a long sling (Tip #46)*

## 46. How to Shorten and Carry Your Long Slings

There are a few different ways to carry long (24-inch/60-centimeter or 48-inch/120-centimeter or longer) slings. Below are the steps for one method that is useful for when you want to carry these slings clipped to your harness (see Figure 8; the sling shown is 48 inches (120 centimeters) long).

Step 1: Fold the sling in half a couple of times to create what looks like a stack of shorter slings.

Step 2: Grab one end of the resulting stack of loops with each hand and twist your hands several times in opposite directions so that the sling starts to contract and bunch up.

Step 3: Bring both ends of the twisted, contracted sling together and clip them both through a carabiner.

## 47. Yet Another Way to Carry Long Slings

This method for making long slings more manageable is exclusively for 48-inch (120-centimeter) slings. Since this particular method is easier to show in a photo than it is to describe with words, just take a look at Figure 9. The benefit to this method is that you can easily unclip one end of the sling from the carabiner and just pull the runner right off. It's much easier than trying to pull it off your shoulders and over your head, especially when you've got a helmet on.

## 48. Should You Build a Trad Rack All at Once or Piece by Piece?

Building a trad rack can seem like a daunting task to the new trad climber. There's just so much to buy! And it's all so expensive! A lot of climbers wonder whether it's best to buy their gear (cams and nuts especially) piece by piece or in sets, and there are pros and cons to each method.

Buying your gear in sets can be cheaper. A full set of nuts, for example, can cost around $90. If you buy each one separately, you'd spend about $120. The same is true for cams. If you buy cams in a set, you'll definitely save money

*Figure 9. Carrying a 48-inch (120-centimeter) sling clipped over the shoulder (Tip #47)*

over buying each one individually. The other main reason to buy in a set is that you've actually got enough gear to go climb something. Try climbing a route with just one cam.

A downside (and it is a big one) to buying your gear in sets is that you might end up with pieces you don't really need. That's why I said that buying your gear in sets can be cheaper. You might find out that you don't need that huge #6 cam after all.

It's hard to plop down $500 or more on gear at one time. If you don't want to wait until you've got all that money saved up, then it's best to buy your gear piece by piece. Though it may be tricky to find routes that you can climb with just a cam or two, there are lots of routes you can climb with three or four cams and a set of nuts (I recommend buying your nuts as a set no matter what). By building your rack piece by piece, you can also better tailor your rack to the area(s) where you climb most often. For example, maybe your local trad crag has a lot of hand-sized cracks, so you can double up on hand sizes and forgo offwidth sizes.

Of course, not everything is so cut and dry. Do you have friends with racks? If so, there's no hurry to amass a huge wad of cams, so buying one cam at a time isn't a big deal. If you don't know anyone else with trad gear, however, it might be best for you to get your gear all at once so that you've got enough gear to climb something.

Everyone's situation is different. If you need all the gear now and have the money for it, get a set of cams. If you don't have the money for a full set, buy a cam or two at a time. If you don't have money for a cam or two at a time, then start making friends with people who have a lot of gear.

## 49. Wear the Right Clothes for Those Offwidths

Whether you love them or hate them, offwidths are part of trad climbing. One key to helping you not despise them quite so much is wearing the proper clothing. It can make a big difference in your comfort level if you wear long pants and a long sleeve shirt. Consider wearing socks if your climbing shoes will still fit with them on. If not, tape up your ankles. And be sure to tape not only your hands but also your wrists. Some rock (like granite) may be more abrasive and painful than others (like sandstone), so keep that in mind too when thinking about how heavily you want to suit up.

## 50. The Old Nut Extension Trick

Here's a trick you can use if the nut placement you're aiming for is a little bit out of reach. Take the nut you want to place and choose another nut that is roughly the same size. Slide the head of the second nut down its wire until it abuts the clip-in loop. Thread the two nuts together as shown in Figure 10 and pull them tight. You now have what is essentially a single long nut that is several inches longer than the original, giving you the extra reach you need to be able to sink that bomber nut placement.

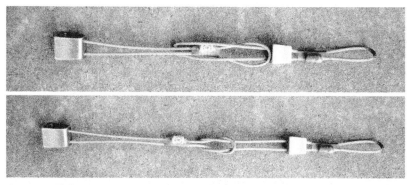

Figure 10. Slide one nut over another and pull tight to help you gain those out-of-reach nut placements. (Tip #50)

# Multi-Pitch Climbing Tips

## 51. Carrying Food When You Don't Have Pockets

I'll often take a couple of protein bars, energy bars, or granola bars with me when I climb a multi-pitch route. They're great for climbing because they still feel and taste the same after they've been squished, melted, and jammed. I like to climb in pants that have a zippered thigh pocket, and this is a perfect place to stash a couple of bars, but sometimes it's just too hot to wear pants, and I end up wearing shorts that don't have a thigh pocket. When this is the case but I still want to take a couple of granola bars with me, I'll cut two 6-inch strips from a roll of duct tape. I'll fold one strip over lengthwise four or five times until it's created a skinny ribbon of tape six inches long. Then I'll use the second piece of tape to attach the ribbon to the wrapper of the granola bar. Voila! I now have a clip-in loop on my snacks. (For years I've made little tape slings for things like lighters and knives, but I only recently had the revelation that they'd work on food items too.)

When the rumbly in your tumbly is too much to bear, open the granola bar from the end that doesn't have the loop on it. Keep the wrapper clipped into the carabiner so you can throw it away once you get back to civilization.

The two strips of tape equal a measly 2-gram addition to your kit. Definitely worth it.

## 52. 6 Things to Consider Before Doing a Multi-Pitch Route

To me, multi-pitch climbing is the essence of the sport. Whether it's a two-pitch sport route at the local crag or a 20-pitch trad line in the mountains, there's just something wonderful about really getting off the ground. The flip side to that, however, is that there are also more things that can go wrong. Here are some things every climber, regardless of skill level, should consider before heading off into the great vertical unknown:

**1. How will you get off?** – Will you be walking off or rappelling down? Will you need two ropes for rappelling? Are you rappelling the line of ascent, or is there a dedicated rappel route? Do you need approach shoes for walking off? If you need to bail mid-route, can you safely and easily do so?

**2. How long should it take, and how long can you afford to take?** – Factor in the approach and descent times and figure out how long each pitch should take. Add it all up and see if you've got enough time. If you lack the experience to know just how long it'll take you, give yourself a generous buffer.

**3. Do you have enough food/water?** – Some of my least pleasant climbing experiences have come from running out of food and water. I can vividly recall running out of water several times on bright white granite slabs in the heat of the summer and developing a horrible case of cottonmouth. I can also recall the time when the zipper of my pants pocket got stuck, and I couldn't access the food inside without cutting my pants open. I was very hungry on that climb.

**4. Do you have the right gear?** – Do you need headlamps? Warm jackets? Any specialty pieces for those massive offwidths and chimneys? Will you need a longer-than-standard rope?

**5. Do you know what you're doing?** – Do some deep soul searching. Do you know what you're doing? Multi-pitch climbing isn't rocket science, but you've got to have your systems dialed. If something goes wrong and you're 500 feet off the deck, you're in for a not-so-grand adventure.

**6. Do you know where the route goes?** – Getting off-route is a great way to get hurt (by knocking off loose rock or climbing into territory more difficult than anticipated) and burn up precious daylight. It's not like a copy of a topo weighs anything. On several occasions I've gotten up on a climb, thinking from looking at the topo or description that the route was obvious, and kicked myself for not remembering where the route went. It's a great way to feel dumb.

# 53. How to Climb Packless

I really, really, really don't like climbing with a pack on. Climbing is all about the freedom and the movement, right? Wearing a pack hinders that freedom and movement. So what is it that would normally go in a pack, and how can you carry it without a pack?

**Food** – This is easy. Wear shorts or pants that have cargo pockets, and stick your food in there.

**Water** – Tape a sling to a water bottle, and clip that to your harness.

**Keys/wallet/phone** – You can stick them in your pockets (ideally you've got shorts or pants with zippered cargo pockets) or the little zipper pocket on your chalk bag (if your chalk bag has one). I have a friend who always hides his keys in bushes or rocks somewhere near the parking lot, and I usually leave my wallet hidden in some hidden nook underneath a seat in my car.

**Approach shoes** – If you're rappelling the route, you won't need to take your approach shoes up the climb with you. If you're going to walk off, however, you've got to take them with you. Most approach shoes have small loops of webbing at the heel that you can clip a carabiner through before clipping the carabiner to your harness. If your shoes don't have that grab loop in the back (or if you've ripped them off like I've done a couple of times), you can clip a carabiner through the shoelaces near the toe. Clip the shoes to one of your rear gear loops or your haul loop.

**Shell jacket** – This one is a bit more difficult. I've taken an extra chalk bag (a clean one with no chalk in it) and stuffed the jacket in there (more in this later). Yeah, it's one more thing hanging off the back of your harness, but at least it's not a backpack. Tying the jacket around your waist is another option if you can manage to do it without it getting in the way of your gear. Ultralight and ultracompact wind jackets are small enough to fit in a standard pocket.

Obviously, all of this will only get you so far. If you're doing something massive like The Nose of El Capitan in a day, for example, either your second will have to wear a pack, or you'll have to haul a small bag. But I've used the systems described here dozens of times, and I think they work for the vast majority of multi-pitch rock climbs out there.

# 54. Set Two Alarms for Early-Morning Starts

A friend and I once went down to Moab for a day of mountain biking. The plan was for him to come pick me up at six in the morning. I woke up at five thirty, got my stuff ready, and had breakfast. Six o'clock came and went. I called my buddy at 6:15. His response was just what I had feared. "Huh? Oh, is it six already?"

I'd like to say that this is an isolated incident and a rare occurrence, but that would be a lie. It's happened fairly often. Maybe I need to get new friends, or maybe my friends just need to use two alarms.

On the behalf of climbing partners everywhere, please, please set two alarms whenever you've got to get up early and someone else is counting on you.

# 55. Pack the Night Before

I once stupidly stayed up late the night before taking a climbing trip. I ended up getting only about three and a half hours of sleep. I woke up the next morning in a zombie-like state and by some miracle managed to pack my harness, shoes, etc. into my backpack. Unfortunately, I forgot my chalk bag, binoculars (we were scoping new lines), and, most unfortunately, my food. Not good. So heed my advice, learn from my mistakes, and pack your bag the night before, when you're still somewhat lucid. If you want to be extra safe, go through all of that stuff again in the morning to make sure you haven't forgotten anything.

## 56. Equalizing Bolted Anchors with 48-Inch (120-Centimeter) Slings

I think the easiest way to make an equalized anchor on a multi-pitch route bolted belays is to use a 48-inch (120-centimeter) sling. This is double the length of a standard over-the-shoulder sling. After arriving at the belay, clip two locking carabiners into the sling and clip a carabiner into each bolt/chain/ring. Arrange the sling into "V" shape and position the point of the "V" so that it's in line with the anticipated direction of pull. Then all you have to do is tie a figure eight on a bight, and you've got a solid, secure anchor. See the first two photos in Figure 11.

The great thing about this setup is that it's light, bomber, and easy to set up.

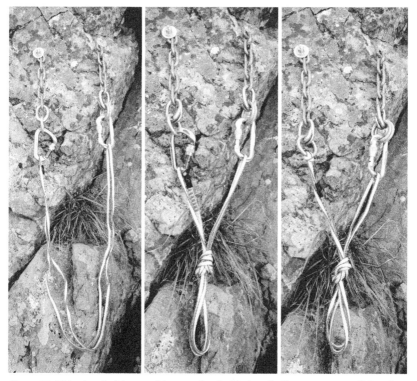

*Figure 11. Using two locking carabiners and a double-length sling to create a solid anchor at a two-bolt belay (first two photos). Girth hitching the left arm of the anchor to the rounded ring of the left bolt (third photo). (Tip #56)*

Yeah, there are many other ways to set up an anchor using quickdraws, the rope, and/or or a couple of shorter slings, but this is my favorite way.

Another thing you could do here if you're short on carabiners is just girth-hitch the sling around one of the anchors, as long as the anchor has a smooth, round surface (like a ring, chain link, or glue-in bolt; you definitely don't want to girth-hitch the sling straight to a bolt hanger). Doing this eliminates the need for a second locking carabiner. See the third photo in Figure 11.

# 57. Take a Tied Sling or Two

You never know why you might need to bail from a multi-pitch route. The weather could turn ugly. You or your partner could get injured. You could get in over your head. Or you could loose your nerve. It's also fairly easy to get off-route and have to rappel or lower off to get back on the route. As such, it's always a good idea to have gear on you to facilitate unforeseen rappels or lowers. Take one or two tied 24-inch (60-centimeter) slings with you. Why tied slings? You can untie them and then tie them around spikes and trees or through holes. They're also cheaper than sewn slings, so you won't feel as bad about leaving them behind.

To tie your own sling, take a 5-foot-long piece of 5/8-inch tubular webbing. Tie it into a loop with a water knot, being sure that the tails on either side of the knot are at least a couple of inches long.

Be prepared to leave a locking carabiner, quick link, or rappel ring on your tied sling when you make that emergency rappel.

# 58. The Mini Water Bottle for Multi-Pitch Routes

I had a minor revelation a couple of years ago. I was unpacking my backpack at home after a six-pitch climb and took out my water bottle. My usual approach to hydration on long climbs like that was to take a 1-liter Nalgene bottle up the route with me, and after that particular climb I noticed that I'd downed less than half of the water in the bottle. I realized how stupid that was. Why take up more water and weight than necessary? Each liter of water weighs a kilogram (2.2 pounds), so I was carrying up (and down) an extra pound of water that I didn't need. Add to that the fact that the large 1-liter bottle often feels a bit unwieldy on the back of my harness, and I realized that it was time for a change. So I went to the gas station down the street and bought the smallest water bottle they had, a tiny little 330 ml (11.16 oz.) container. I then grabbed some duct tape and a small loop of thin cord (webbing would work too), and it wasn't long before I had a perfect little water bottle to hang from my harness. See Figure 13.

I used it a couple of days later on an eight-pitch route, and it was perfect. Even that smaller amount of water was more than I needed. I also really liked its small size on my harness. In case you were wondering if that's all I drank the whole day, the answer is no. I still took a 1-liter bottle with me to drink from on the approach and descent (about 45 minutes each way).

Now, let me write a disclaimer here. I don't know how much water you need to survive or be comfortable. That 330 ml is enough for me for eight pitches in the shade in relatively cool temperatures. Don't go buy a tiny water bottle, take it on a climb with you, die, and haunt me. I absolve myself from any responsibility.

Figure 12. A tiny water bottle for taking up multi-pitch routes (Tip #58)

## 59. Rope Management on Multi-Pitch Routes

Proper rope management is essential when climbing multi-pitch routes. The last thing you want is for your leader to be strung out on a sketchy lead when you realize there's a massive tangled knot creeping its way toward your belay device. Ideally there's a ledge at the belay so that as you're belaying your second up, you can neatly stack the rope on the ledge. When that's not the case, use the method I describe here.

Let's back up a little bit. When you get to the belay and set up an equalized anchor, you clip yourself into the power point of the anchor, right? This is often done with a clove hitch (my preferred method) on the lead rope or maybe a sling or two. So you've got the rope going from the tie-in point on your harness to the power point of the anchor, and the rope continues on down to your

*Figure 13. Flake the rope over your tether as you belay your second up (Tip #59)*

belayer from there.

So back to rope management. As you bring your belayer up, flake the rope that you're taking in over the bit of rope that goes from you to the power point. Flake a few feet (a meter) or so of rope over each side at a time, going back and forth. See Figure 13. Whether you connect to the anchor via the rope or via a sling or two, the general principle of flaking the rope from side to side is the same.

After you've belayed your second all the way up to where you are, and as he/she starts leading the next pitch, you've got to make sure you pay the rope out smoothly and that the rope still doesn't get tangled. If you're not switching leads—that is, if you'll also be leading the next pitch—you'll have to transfer the load of rope from one person to the other. One way to avoid this potentially messy task is to use a long sling specifically for this purpose of managing the rope (instead of using the section of rope between your harness and the anchor). Then all you'd have to do is unclip the end of the sling attached to you and clip it to your belayer.

# 60. Always Have a Small Headlamp With You

A buddy and I put up a new long route in an obscure canyon, and we didn't start hiking in till about 4:15 in the afternoon. The approach involved horrendous bushwhacking, the climb was a lot longer than we thought it would be, and the descent required some involved downclimbing. In other words, it was the perfect recipe for a major epic.

Fortunately, we made it back to the trail at the bottom of the canyon just as it was getting too dark to see where we were going. We were lucky. The whole afternoon, I was thinking how stupid I was for not bringing a small headlamp. I have a tiny one that I originally bought for night running, but now I stick it in my pocket or pack if it looks like there's any chance at all that I'll be caught out in the dark. I recommend you do the same. If you don't want to take a headlamp, even a single-LED keychain light is far better than nothing.

# 61. Use an Extra Chalk Bag to Carry Stuff on a Long Route

As stated earlier, I hate climbing with a pack. I very rarely climb with a pack, instead opting to go light and have everything on my harness. Last year I climbed a 14-pitch route and faced a problem. I knew the morning was going to be cold but also that the temperature would get up into the 80s (about 27+ degrees Celsius) by mid-day. I needed a jacket for the first part of the day but didn't know what to do with it once it got warmer.

I decided to use an empty (and clean) chalk bag. I stuffed my jacket in when the day got hot, and I also managed to fit a small headlamp and a couple of Clif Bars in there. I was carrying my chalk bag on a webbing belt, and I just slid the extra chalk bag on the same belt. It worked really well, and I didn't even notice it on my harness.

# 62. Lightning Safety Tips for Climbers

Lightning kills about 300 people each year in the US alone. The good news is that if you or someone in your group gets struck, you or they have a 66% chance of living. The bad news is that you or they have a 34% chance of dying.

Obviously, you want to check the weather forecast before you hike or climb. Also, make sure you understand the general weather patterns of the areas you're going to be in. Alpine areas, for example, often have afternoon thunderstorms. Be aware of what the weather is doing. Look around and check the horizon often. Is there a storm or clouds coming? Storms generally move at about 20 miles (32 kilometers) an hour, so you can't outrun then.

Measure the time between lightning strikes and thunder claps. Divide the number of seconds by 5, and that's how many miles away the storm is. For example, a 5-second gap between the lightning and thunder indicate that the storm is 1 mile away.

Here are some more tips for hiking and climbing in lightning storms:

**Avoid these things:** Metal, water, high places, solitary tall trees, close contact with others, open spaces, changes in terrain (areas of contact between dissimilar objects, like rock and ground, tree and ground, land and water, etc.), narrow areas that could be dangerous in the event of a flash flood.

**Look for these things:** A low stand of trees, areas of low ground like ditches or trenches.

**Other things to keep in mind:** Leave your pack containing any metal at least 100 feet away. Crouch down, lower your head, cover your ears with your hands, and close your eyes. Injured people don't retain the electrical charge, so it's safe to touch them. If you see a thunderstorm coming while you're climbing, it's usually better to bail and rappel than push through and go to the top of the route or mountain.

Oh, and lightning can indeed strike twice.

# 63. How to Belay Your Second Up (from Above) With a Grigri

On multi-pitch or long single-pitch routes, I usually belay my second up with an auto-blocking tube-style belay device in guide mode, but I occasionally (and stupidly) forget to bring it with me. On one such occasion, I happened to have my Petzl Grigri with me and figured I'd give it a try. The result? I really liked it! At this time, I was climbing on a fatter rope (10.3 mm) that usually took a bit of muscle to wrangle through the tube-style belay device, but it was smooth sailing with the Grigri.

How do you set this up? Well, let's assume that you've already built an anchor, clipped in to it, and brought up all of the slack in the rope. You're now ready to put your partner on belay so he/she can start climbing up. Set up the Grigri like you would for any normal lead or toprope belay (making sure, of course, that the rope is correctly threaded through the device). The side that always goes to the climber when you're belaying a leader from the ground is the same side of the rope that goes down to the climber that you're belaying up to you.

Then all you have to do is clip the locking carabiner into the power point of your anchor. See Figure 14. In the image, the right side of the rope is going down to the climber.

As the climber climbs up, just take in all the slack. If the climber falls or

*Figure 14. A Grigri set up to belay a climber from above. The left side of the rope in this photo goes to the climber. (Tip #63)*

puts weight the rope, the Grigri locks up and prevents any rope from slipping through. The weight of the climber goes entirely on the anchor, not onto you. Pretty slick.

Keep in mind that if your route requires you to make rappels, it's still best to bring along some kind of rappel device that works on double-rope rappels since the Grigri does not.

# 64. Always Take More Beta Than You Think You'll Need

Before I did the East Face of Mt. Whitney (a classic rock route in the High Sierra in California) several summers ago, I found a topo of the route online. It looked pretty good, so I printed it out and took it with me on the route. I didn't bother taking any other info up. Well, I got up on the route and realized that the topo wasn't quite as good as I thought it was. In fact, it was very inaccurate. We ended up wasting a lot of time on the route trying to find the right line.

This has happened to me over and over again, and I've finally wised up a bit. I now take with me all of the information I can find, especially for long approaches and tricky descents. On your computer, copy all of the info you can find and paste it into a blank document. Make the text and margins really small, print on both sides of the page, and you should be able to condense all information onto a single piece of paper.

# Gear Tips

# 65. 6 Ways to Score Cheap Gear

The beautiful thing about climbing is that it's a relatively cheap hobby—once you have the gear. Climbing gear, while worth the money we pay for it, can seem freakishly expensive if you're just starting out. You can spend thousands of dollars on gear and still have a list of thousands of dollars-worth that you still want to buy. Luckily, there are some great ways to save yourself some cash. Here are six:

1. eBay – eBay isn't as good of a place to score cheap gear as you might think. The problem is that there are tons of people out there who want exactly what you want. As such, it's generally hard to get really good deals (though I've found it to be a great place to sell gear because you get top dollar). There are ways, though. I once got myself a sweet bivy sack that had been used only once. This bad boy retailed for $220ish, but I got it for $80. How? The seller spelled it "bivi" instead of "bivy." People searching for it normally wouldn't be able to find it. The overall best way of going about trying to get deals is to go browse through gear categories manually instead of searching for terms.

2. **Outlet/deal websites** – Sites like REI Garage (*http://www.rei.com/rei-garage*), Steep and Cheap (*http://steepandcheap.com*), and Sierra Trading Post (*http://sierratradingpost.com*), among many others, can have great deals (though often they're short on climbing gear and longer on clothing, so you need to check often and be patient). Go to the normal big online gear retailers (Moosejaw, Backcountry.com, Mountain Gear, etc.) and click on their sales pages. If you want to know when these places have sales, sign up for their email newsletters.

3. **Comparison shopping** – Use Google's Product Search functionality (*http://www.google.com/shopping*) or other price comparison engines to search for whatever gear you want, and then sort the results by price from lowest to highest.

4. **Forums** – There are several climbing websites that have forums. These include Mountain Project (*http://mountainproject.com*), Summitpost (*http://summitpost.org*), SuperTopo (*http://supertopo.com*), and RockClimbing.com. People are always selling gear, and some of these forums even have dedicated sub-forums for buying and selling gear. I've found that this is one of the best ways to get cheap stuff.

5. **Gear swaps** – If you live in an area with lots of climbers, there are probably some gear swaps that go on from time to time throughout the year. In Salt Lake City, for example, Black Diamond hosts a gear swap twice a year, once in the spring and once in the fall. In my experience, this is the number one best way of getting cheap gear. You can handle and inspect the gear yourself (which you can't do before buying gear online) and maybe even haggle. I've gotten a pair of

Black Diamond ice tools for $30, an ice axe for $10, and cams for $5.

**6. Classifieds** – Craigslist (*http://craigslist.org*) and similar classified websites often have good deals. There are also gear-specific classifieds like GearTrade (*http://geartrade.com*).

And finally, I guess you could always get sponsored, but uh… that's definitely easier said than done. Don't bet on it happening. Also, if you've got gear you don't need anymore but are short on cash, consider offering it as a trade for something else.

# 66. A Fun Way to Store Gear

I usually store all of my gear in a couple of big plastic bins, but it's kind of a pain having to wade through it all to find what I'm looking for. I came up with a storage alternative that also displays the gear in a fun way, and it's essentially a rack that leans up against the wall. See Figure 15.

The sides of the rack are two vertically oriented 1-inch (25-millimeter) PVC pipes. Gear is clipped onto lengths of 5/16-inch (9-millimeter) threaded that is installed perpendicular to the pipes. The whole thing cost less than $20 to make, and the only tools required are a saw to cut the pipe and a drill to drill 5/16-inch holes into the PVC. I love it because it's really easy to find what I've got. Plus I just enjoy looking at my gear. I've had 4 sets of cams, 100+ biners, and a ton of draws on it all at once, and it held up just fine.

*Figure 15. Using a homemade rack to store and display gear (Tip #66)*

This type of gear storage doesn't work well for me in the summer and other times that I'm climbing a lot because my rack usually stays in my pack, but even then it's still great for storing and displaying the gear that I don't use every time I go out.

## 67. The Perfect Chalk Bag

Huh? What difference does it make? Aren't all chalk bags the same? Does it matter what kind you've got? At the end of the day, no, it doesn't really matter a whole lot. A chalk bag's most important function is to hold your chalk, and every chalk bag on the market can at least do that. But there are several chalk bag features that can make your climbing life easier. Let me describe the elements of my ideal chalk bag:

**Tight closure** – Chalk bags hold chalk. If they don't do that well, they fail their main purpose. If a chalk bag is pretty but it lets chalk get all over everything else in your bag, that's no good. (If your chalk bag leaks, stuff it in a Ziploc bag before sticking it into your pack or the trunk of your car.)

**Easy closure** – I don't want anything too fancy or complicated, and I want it to stay open for easy hand dipping. Is that too much to ask?

**Good size** – The perfect chalk bag needs to swallow my whole hand, not just lightly dust my fingers.

**Brush holder** – I don't use it very often, but once in a while it's nice to have a brush handy. Other climbers I know use theirs all the time. Either way, make sure your chalk bag has a loop or sleeve of some sort that will hold a brush.

**Small pocket** – Most chalk bags don't have a little pocket on them, but I love the ones that do. It doesn't really matter on single pitch routes, but it's nice to have a place to put keys, matches, or an energy bar for longer routes.

## 68. 7 Things to Look for in a Climbing Knife

It's always a good idea to take a knife with you on long routes. The knife makes it easier to cut and replace tattered, sun-bleached webbing. A good climbing knife should (1) be light, (2) be small, (3) have a locking blade, (4) be easy to clip onto a carabiner, (5) be easy to open with one hand, (6) not be able to open unexpectedly while on a harness, and (7) be sharp.

Sure, there are specially made climbing knives (the Trango and Petzl ones come to mind), but they're a bit pricey. I ended up making my own for a grand total of $2. Which brings me to…

# 69. The $2 Climbing Knife

I bought a cheap little knife at a generic sporting goods store. The knife had a couple key features that I wanted, namely a belt clip and a hole that I could put a key ring through. I took a piece of 1-inch (25-centimeter) flat webbing, wrapped it around the knife, and sewed it into a loop. When slipped around the knife, this loop prevents the knife from opening, and the belt clip keeps the webbing loop in place. The key ring makes it easy to attach the knife to a carabiner. The final product is really simple but really effective. The knife is lightweight and sharp enough to cut through old webbing. Not bad for $2. See Figure 16.

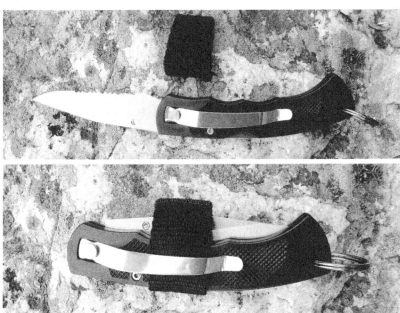

*Figure 16. The $2 climbing knife (Tip #69)*

# 70. 5 Ways to Mark the Middle of Your Rope

There are three reasons why it's important to have the middle of your rope marked. First, it's easy to set up single-rope rappels; I can think of few things worse than misjudging where the middle of the rope is and ending high up above the ground or the next set of rappel anchors. Second, when toproping, you can visually see where the middle is so you can make sure the toproped climber has enough rope to get back down to the ground. And third, when leading, the belayer can yell up to the climber and tell him/her that half of the rope is left. This is helpful for the climber to know when he/she is on a multi-pitch climb and needs to find a good place to create an anchor and set up the belay, or when he/she is thinking of combining pitches.

There are several ways to mark the middle of a rope:

**1. Permanent marker** – My preferred way of marking the middle of the rope is to take a marker and make a solid band of black at the rope's midpoint. Some rope manufacturers make markers specifically for use on ropes. If those aren't available to you, don't use a normal Sharpie permanent marker; use a laundry marker instead. These are water-based permanent markers made specifically for writing on fabric, and they're super cheap (you can get one for a dollar or two; I got mine at Walmart). The black mark that you make on the rope does fade with time and use. I usually have to mark the middle twice for each rope before it gets retired.

**2. Dental floss** – Well, I guess it doesn't have to be dental floss; you can use any strong, synthetic thread. Whatever you use, find a bright color that will contrast with the rope. What you want to do is thread the floss through a needle and make several passes through the sheath of the rope. Some say it's important to not go through the core of the rope; I doubt it would make a difference, but do whatever you feel comfortable with. I have a climbing partner who uses floss on his ropes, and it's a pretty good system. It's easy to do and easy to see, plus it seems to last a while.

**3. Tape** – You can use duct tape, electrical tape, or sports tape. Just use a little; a thick roll of tape around the rope will prevent it from fitting through a belay device! This is not a very permanent solution, though that might not be a bad thing if, for example, you have to cut off the ends of your rope at some point and need to re-mark the middle point. I've climbed on ropes that are marked like this and personally don't like it much both because of the extra stiffness and bulk it creates and because it may leave behind a sticky residue if you choose to remove it, but at least it's quick and easy.

**4. Dental floss (again)** – Some people wrap the floss around the middle of the rope instead of using a needle to sew it through. This seems like it would work fine, but it also seems like more work than some of the other options.

**5. Buy a bi-pattern rope** – OK, so this isn't really a way for you to mark a rope, but you can get ropes that have two different colors or patterns on them; the pattern changes in the middle. This is awesome, but it adds more cost to an already expensive piece of gear.

# 71. The Easy Way to Clean Your Rope

You know what I hate? I hate my hands being covered in black nastiness after belying with a dirty rope. Luckily, cleaning a rope is a pretty darn easy thing to do.

It's simple. Put your rope in a washing machine and wash it. Do not use the type of washing machine that most people have in their houses; the rope will wrap around the plastic agitator thing in the middle and mess it up. Go to a laundromat instead and use one of the front-loading washing machines. Don't put any soap in, and wash it in cold water. Some people say that you can use a mild soap without damaging the rope, but washing it without soap gets it clean enough for me.

I've also heard of people putting their ropes in mesh bags and then putting the mesh bag in the washer. I've never done it, but it seems that that would work well for making sure the rope doesn't get worked into one giant knot.

Dry your rope in a place out of direct sunlight. I usually do it in my shower, draping it over the shower rod and/or along the sides of the tub. It works well.

# 72. The Beauty of Trekking Poles

I remember when I first saw trekking poles. They were in Backpacker magazine, and it was sometime in the late 1990s. I distinctly remember thinking, "That is the dumbest thing I've ever seen. What a gimmick!" The article mentioned something about how the trekking poles take some significant percentage of the weight off of your knees and how they let you do a variety of activities better and easier. Psha. Whatever. That's all just marketing fluff, right?

Fast-forward a decade. I'd been climbing, hiking, and mountaineering for a number of years by then, and over that decade, two things had happened to change my perception of trekking poles.

The first was that while I was in great shape and could fly up mountains, coming down them sucked. My knees were getting hammered, and they hurt. Because of the pain in my knees, I was no faster coming down mountains and trails than I was going up.

The second was that I started carrying heavier and heavier loads in my pack, which also helped destroy my knees. Climbing gear is heavy, and all of that extra weight puts a lot of strain on the knees.

Going downhill and heavy packs. Those were the two things that caused me to change my mind about trekking poles. I broke down and got a pair. And let me tell you, they made life a lot easier. I could go downhill faster and carry the heavy loads without pulverizing my knees. On top of that, I've found that I

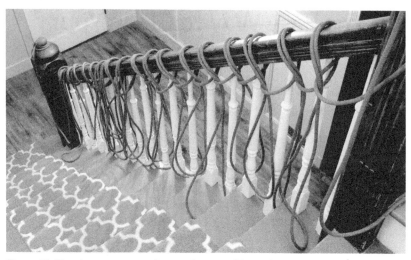

*Figure 17. Hanging a rope up to dry on a banister (Tip #73)*

often do hike faster with trekking poles. They're definitely gear that I'm happy to have handed over my hard-earned money for.

# 73. Another Way to Dry a Climbing Rope

When I was living in a house with a bunch of my buddies while in college, I'd often drape the rope on the shower rod or on the side of the bathtub. The problem was that the shower was used a lot, leaving little time for the rope to dry. I realized that using the handrail along the stairway worked just as well, drying out completely in about a day. See Figure 17.

Another good option that I've seen other people use is to set up an ironing board and lay the rope out to dry on that.

# 74. How to Loosen a Stubborn Knot

Got a really stubborn knot that's impossible to untie? Try tapping it with a hammer or rock, turning the knot as you hit it so that you strike the knot on all sides. Before too long the stubborn knot will loosen right up. Don't whack the webbing (or rope or cord) too hard, obviously, and don't use any jagged rocks for the hammering.

## 75. Painful Climbing Shoes Are Bad

For years I climbed in shoes that were too tight for me. Everything I read and everything I heard stated that climbing shoes have to hurt or else you won't climb well in them. That's just the way it was, and you had to deal with it.

When I started climbing seriously—and therefore started spending more and more time in my shoes—I realized that it just wasn't worth it. I went to the local climbing shop and tried on every single pair in the place (more 20 different pairs in all) until I found a pair that I could cinch down pretty darn tight without my toes screaming in pain. The next time I hit the crags, I took my new shoes. I thought that I would notice a huge negative difference in my ability. Well, guess what. I didn't. In fact, I actually climbed better because I was having more fun and because my toes didn't feel like they were going to fall off. Instead of having to gingerly place my toe on a hold, I could just fire away and stand on anything without pain. Eureka!

So don't buy a pair of shoes just because of their super wicked aggro down-camber. Buy shoes because they fit well, because they are comfortable. That's the trick. It is possible to go too far to the other extreme. Shoes that are three sizes too big may be comfortable, but you're not going to climb well in them.

Keep in mind that different brands and styles fit people's feet differently. I'm a La Sportiva guy because their shoes tend to fit the shape of my foot better. Your mileage will vary.

Whether you're looking for an all-day shoe or a hardcore bouldering shoe, try enough different pairs on and you'll eventually find something that just sucks on to your feet perfectly and doesn't hurt too much (unless you have weird feet; then I don't know what to tell you). If you're trying a shoe on in the store and have to walk around on the outside edge of your foot because it's too painful to apply pressure to your toes, do you really think that'll translate well to using your toes to get up a rock climb? No. Buy shoes that fit well and you'll be a better, happier climber.

## 76. Finding the Middle of a Rope That Has No Middle Marker

You can still easily find the middle of your rope if it's not marked (or if it's dark and you can't see anything). Grab both ends together so they're even and starting flaking or coiling both strands of the rope at the same time, moving toward the middle. You'll eventually run out of rope to flake, and that's when you've found the middle. This is also how you can find the middle of the rope to mark it in the first place.

## 77. Tie a Knot in Your Shoelaces

It's really annoying when the laces of your climbing shoes come out of their holes. And it's even more annoying when you can't put them back in again because the little plastic tube that holds the end together has come off. You might as well be trying to shove a handful of boiled spaghetti noodles through a keyhole. The solution? Simply tie a knot in the end of your shoelaces so that they can't come out in the first place.

## 78. How to Jumpstart a Car With Climbing Gear

I went into the local climbing store the other day and heard a funny story. After a long, hard, hot day of climbing, my friend and his partner returned to their car and found their battery dead. Fortunately, there were a few passing cars that they flagged down with the hope of getting a jumpstart. Unfortunately, no one had jumper cables. Then one of the climbers had an idea. Why not string a bunch of nuts together to connect the batteries?

And guess what. It worked! How cool is that? The lesson from this story is twofold. First, always have jumper cables and other essential safety items in your car. And second, a little bit of ingenuity with gear can get you out of sticky situations even when you're not on the rock.

## 79. The Chalk Funnel

Making a funnel out of a piece of paper makes it easier to fill up your chalk ball with loose chalk without getting it all over you. Figure 18 illustrates the three-step process.

Step 1: Fold a piece of paper in half lengthwise.

Step 2: Roll one end of the folded paper to form a cone.

Step 3: Stick the end of the cone into the chalk ball and pour loose chalk through the open end of the funnel.

## 80. Buy the Best Gear

Black Diamond once did a test of some cheap Ukrainian climbing gear that is readily available online. They tested a bunch of cams, carabiners, and nuts. The

*Figure 18. Making a paper cone to fill a chalk ball with loose chalk (Tip #79)*

result was that they all broke below their stated rating. Now, the ratings they broke at weren't horrible. Indeed, they broke at strengths higher than several of the smaller Black Diamond cams. The carabiners tested were actually stronger than stated and stronger than Black Diamond's carabiners.

So if you're in the market for gear, should you go out and get a bunch of Ukrainian gear off eBay? I think not. While these particular cams were "strong enough," they went through no certification process. There is no quality control. Who knows if the next cam you buy will fail at 2 or 12 kN? Cams from a reputable company have gone through a stringent safety process and are certified to hold to at least their stated strength.

I actually have two of those Ukrainian cams. I bought them when I was in Ukraine several years ago. They were $7 each. I've never used them, never taken them on a climb with me, and I never will. I bought them more as souvenirs than anything else. They are not nice cams. The action is funky, the stem is limp, and they just feel cheap overall. For me, the ability to climb hard above gear hinges on my faith in my gear. You think I want a $7 cam between me and an early death? No way.

When you're paying $70 for a cam, you're paying for peace of mind. That brings me to my point: buy the best gear, even if you have to wait a little bit longer to be able to afford it. Buy quality gear that will perform well and last a long time. Don't get some crappy no-name cams because they're $20 cheaper per cam than a Camalot, Dragon, or Friend.

Buying the best gear first will actually save you money in the long run. You'll realize a year or so into your trad climbing career that your ghetto cams suck and that you want nicer ones. If you end up buying them eventually, you might as well buy them first.

*Figure 19. A quick link on a harness haul loop (Tip #81)*

# 81. Always Have a Quick Link on Your Harness

I like to always have a quick link on my harness. As shown in Figure 19, I keep it attached to my haul loop, which I very rarely use for anything else. It's great to always have one of these with you because you don't have to leave a carabiner or draw when bailing off a sport route, you can replace worn anchor hardware if you need to, and you don't have to leave a more valuable locking carabiner on a webbing rap anchor.

Sure, a quick link is a little bit heavier than a regular carabiner, but it's also cheaper. It never gets in the way when it's on my harness, and I never even notice that it's there. I recommend spray-painting it beforehand to minimize visual impact if/when you do use it.

# 82. The Beauty of Sunglasses

Until very recently, I had never owned a pair of real sunglasses. I remember getting $3 sunglasses at gas stations when I was a kid. I also had several pairs of fake Oakleys over the years. I have a pair of glacier glasses that I use on snowy peaks and at higher elevations, but I always thought that regular sunglasses were overrated. Just suck it up and squint, you baby. I'd rather spend the money on a cam or two.

All of this changed when I had some extra cash and decided it was time to try real sunglasses. I figured that if I was going to spend $50 or $100 on the things, I'd at least get some that looked decent on me. And because I have no fashion sense whatsoever, I brought a friend's wife along as a fashion consultant to tell me what looked good and what didn't. I tried on every pair in the store and finally found a pair I loved.

Now I'm quick to sing the praises of sunglasses. It really is very nice not having to squint. I can climb without having to use my hand to shield my eyes from the sun. My eyes don't burn as much at the end of a long day in the mountains. They're nice to have when driving into the sun. They keep bugs and mud out of my eyes when mountain biking. They keep rock and metal out of my eyes when I'm drilling holes and pounding bolts.

So I've been converted. I'm a believer. My sunglasses were $60 and probably the single best gear purchase I've made in the last year. In fact, it's hard to think of a single piece of outdoor gear that's had more of an overall positive impact on the quality my life. I wish I'd gotten them sooner.

# 83. Unscrewing a Stuck Locking Carabiner

Sometimes it's really hard to unscrew a locking carabiner once it's been weighted. Try as hard as you might, you can't unscrew the stupid thing. If that happens to you, just try weighting it again and unscrewing it while it's weighted. That should do the trick.

# 84. Climb on Both Ends of Your Rope

Don't always climb on the same end of your rope. When you always use the same end to tie in and climb on, the rope wears unevenly. Your rope will last longer if you alternate the end that you climb on.

# 85. Use a Length of Cord As a Chalk Bag Belt

When I lost my chalk bag not too long ago, I had a spare but no webbing belt for it. I did have some extra 5-millimeter cord, so I used that. And you know what?

*Figure 20. Using a length of 5-millimeter cord as a chalk bag belt (Tip #85)*

I really like it. I secure it with either a flat overhand knot or a square knot, and it feels more secure than a normal plastic buckle. The main reason I like the cord belt is that it can be used to tie an emergency prusik knot. I don't normally carry a prusik cord, but having one as a chalk bag belt gives me a little extra peace of mind. See Figure 20.

## 86. When Should You Leave Gear Behind?

For aesthetic and financial reasons, you always want to remove any gear that you place. But is there ever a time you should leave gear? Yes. Here are six situations when you might have to:

1. If you need to leave rappel anchors, you'll have to part with some gear. Before you do this, look all around you to see if someone has already put in bolts, put slings around a tree, or left a couple of nuts. If not, is there a boulder or horn you can loop the rope or a piece of webbing around? If the route has been done before, chances are good that someone else has rappelled off of it before (unless you can walk off).

2. Sometimes a piece gets stuck. Maybe a cam has walked back and is overcammed, or you've fallen on a nut and it's welded itself into the crack. If you and

your partner have the time, then by all means spend as much time as necessary to remove your stuck gear. If bad weather is approaching, if you have lots of vertical feet above you to cover still, or if you have some other time constraints, you might be better off just leaving the gear where it is. You can try getting your gear back by posting notes at the parking lot or on online clibing forums, but the general rule is that if you leave it, it's fair game for the next climber that comes across it.

3. You might need to leave gear if you bail off of a trad route. It's better to leave a few nuts and a cam behind on that 2,000-foot-long (600-meter-long) alpine ridge than get struck by lightning and die.

4. You'll have to leave a carabiner or two (or the aforementioned quick link from tip #81) when lowering off of a sport route that's too hard for you, though it's better to hangdog your way to the anchors if at all possible so that you don't have to leave anything behind.

5. When following a long pendulum, you'll need to leave something behind to lower off from

6. When a ring or chain link at an anchor looks very worn, add a few points to your karma jar by replacing the bad chain or link. Again, a quick link is great for this.

# 87. 16 Things to Do With an Old Rope

I go through about a rope a year and always have old bits of rope floating around. They're under my bed, in storage, in my trunk, in the back seat of my car. If you find yourself in a similar situation, here are 16 useful things you can do with them:

**1. Make a rug** – This is a classic old standby that just about everyone seems to want to do but few of us actually end up doing. There are two types of constructing rope rugs, the kind where you knot or weave the rope (*http://www.summitpost.org/so-you-want-to-make-a-rope-rug-eh/263578*) and the kind where you circle the rope around and around in a spiral (*http://www.instructables.com/id/Rope-Rug/*) and then use tape and glue to hold it together. I've also heard of people sewing rope rugs, though I've never seen one.

**2. Sell it** – You can get a few bucks by selling your old rope on eBay or Craigslist. I saw an old rope recently sell on eBay for $46. Not bad!

3. **Make dog leashes** – Take old Fido for a walk and look stylin' while doing it.

4. **Use it as a snow rope** – A rope that you don't want to use for lead climbing can still continue its purpose as a rope for glacier travel or traversing a steep snow slope. Usually these types of ropes are half the length of a standard rope (like 30 meters long rather than 60 meters).

5. **Use it as a TR rope** – The forces generated in toproping are much smaller than those in lead climbing, so most old climbing ropes can still do work as a dedicated toprope line. You can cut a longer rope into sections if the cliffs you toprope on are short.

6. **Donate it to a scout troop** – So they can practice tying knots and stuff.

7. **Make miscellaneous trinkets** – You can make dog/cat toys (search online for "climbing rope dog toy" or something similar), key chains, and other little incidentals.

8. **Use it as a towrope** – Throw that old rope in your trunk, along with some beater booty 'biners (say that three times fast) and you've got an emergency towing setup. Old static ropes are best for this.

9. **Put it in as a fixed rope on sketchy ascent/descent** – A number of areas have ropes fixed on difficult or sketch sections of the approach or on scrambling sections between tiers of rock on a multi-pitch route. Be a friend to the climbing community and replace those nasty old things.

10. **Use it as a skip rope or jump rope** – Good for you to get in shape with or for the kids to play on.

11. **Make a rope swing** – If there's a local watering hole that you or the local kids enjoy, consider creating a rope swing or replacing the old rope swings.

12. **Make a rope ladder** – Like the one at *http://www.ehow.com/how_4443215_make-rope-ladder.html*. Good for a tree house and whatever else your mind can dream up.

13. **Make it into a slackline?** – Are there people who slackline on rope? I don't know, but maybe you should give it a try. I bet it would hurt the feet, though. If nothing else, you could maybe use it as a backup line to a highline.

14. **Use it as a beater rope** – I often use my old ropes as sturdy workhorse ropes. For example, I fix them on routes that I'm cleaning and prepping. All the jugging up and rapping down (plus all the dirt getting into the sheath and the loose blocks smashing the rope below) is not what I want to do on a nice, new rope.

15. **Ask around and donate it to whoever wants it** – I know the guys at my local climbing shop are always looking for ropes for their various projects. Ask around and see if anyone is interested.

16. **Make a Bachar ladder** – This is an old school training gizmo, kind of like a rope ladder, but usually made with PVC rungs and hung at an angle. Search online for "Bachar ladder" and you'll find more photos and information.

17. **Make art** – A quick online image search for "climbing rope art" brings up great examples works of art made from climbing ropes by people with far more talent than me.

# Training and Downtime Tips

## 88. A Fun Climbing Game for the Gym

I don't really like climbing in the gym. It is a shallow reflection of everything that I love about climbing. But I recently got a free month-long membership to the local gym and need to get stronger after a long, lazy winter.

A friend and I were in the gym's bouldering section. We had done the marked problems we wanted to do, so we were just messing around with dynos and big reaches. This evolved into a game where we tried to get to the top of the wall using as few holds as possible. We got to the point where we could use just three holds.

You could do this on bouldering walls, climbing walls, or even on real rock. The next time you're stuck in the grim sanctuary that is the gym, try it out. It'll help tide you over till you can get back on the real stuff.

## 89. The $20 Hangboard Alternative

Hangboards are expensive and a pain to mount, especially if you're renting the place you live in and don't want to deal with having to patch up any holes you put in the wall. A couple of months ago, I bought one of those pull-up bars that attaches to a standard doorframe. You don't have to drill any holes, and it leaves no marks. No, it's not as good as a hangboard for climbing-specific training, but it is a lot cheaper and easier to deal with. The thing is easily detachable, and you can use it to do pushups and sit-ups too.

## 90. 7 Climbing Skills You Can Practice

I was talking to a friend the other day about slacklining. He said he didn't like it because he wasn't any good at it. I told him that no one is good at it when they first try it and that the key is just practicing a ton until it gets easier or until you get better.

As I was thinking about this, I realized that the same applies to climbing. You hear a lot about practicing for other sports, but not so much for climbing, and I realized that there are a lot of things in climbing that you can practice. Here are some I came up with:

1. Practice tying knots.

2. Practice clipping your rope into a quickdraw.

3. Practice dynos. They can be pretty scary to do on the rock if you're not familiar with them, so consider practicing them in the gym on toprope.

4. Practice placing cams and nuts at ground level.

5. Practice the anchor-cleaning process on the ground. Sling some table legs and use them as your anchor points.

6. If a certain kind of climbing hold gives you trouble (slopers, sidepulls, etc.), practice climbing on routes that have lots of those holds.

7. Practice a route's moves when you're not on the route. Work through the beta with your hands and feet so you'll have the moves dialed once you get back on the route.

# 91. A Few Words About Recovery Time

Climbing is great, but being in pain while climbing significantly lessens the enjoyment. I once hurt my foot while running and whenever I walked, I had a sharp pain on the lower outer side of my left foot. I kept off it for a few days but then went back to climbing and hiking as usual. Eventually the pain mostly went away, though every so often I'd take a bad step and the pain would come back for a bit. Then I very unwisely ran a marathon and screwed it up all over again.

The marathon also gave me a case of shin splints. I was in pretty severe pain for a couple days there, but after that the pain wasn't bad enough to keep me from walking. I then went to a park and tossed a baseball around with a friend. I wasn't doing a whole lot of intense running or anything, but I had to jump a few times to catch the ball and jog after the missed ball every once in a while. My legs hurt a little more after that, but it still wasn't excruciating. I didn't worry about it too much.

I went climbing again after two weeks. The approach to the cliff took about an hour and my foot and shins were hurting a little, but again, not so much to keep me from doing what I love. The four-pitch climb didn't hurt too much, either, but walking back on the trail hurt more than the approach. (Stay with me here, I promise this is all leading to something.)

I then went mountain biking and had to stick my leg out a couple times to keep me up when I had some minor crashes. This was definitely not good for my shins, and I definitely felt the pain. It was more painful to walk after that than it had been since the day after the marathon.

In other words, I wasn't getting any better.

This is a problem of mine. I hate downtime. I hate not climbing and not being outside. I expect that a lot of you are the same way. But let me just say that being perpetually injured sucks way more than not climbing. If you're hurting, take time off until you feel 100% better, until your body has healed itself completely. The rocks (and mountains and trails and so forth) will always be there. Sure, you might be able to grin and bear it, but why? Apart from the unpleasantness of the pain itself, it will keep you from performing at the level you were accustomed to before. Busy yourself with activities that don't require the use of your injured parts.

# 92. 12 Climbing-Related Things to Waste Your Time on When You Can't Climb

Most of us don't get out climbing as often as we'd like. Sometimes schedules won't allow it, sometimes the weather doesn't cooperate, and sometimes injury prevents it. Here's a list of climbing-related things you can occupy yourself with when you're stuck inside:

1. Add more routes to your to-do list by browsing through Mountain Project (*http://mountainproject.com*). Check out climbs and areas in states and countries that you've never been to before.

2. Play CyberClimber (*http://cyberclimber.com*) or any other climbing-related game you can find.

3. Sort through and organize your gear.

4. Sell any gear you don't need.

5. Read an adventure- or climbing-related book.

6. Browse through the archives on climbing magazine websites.

7. Read and comment on climbing blogs or climbing forums.

8. Write about your climbing (mis)adventures. Maybe even start a climbing blog.

9. Organize your climbing photos.

10. Go to SummitPost (*http://summitpost.org*) and look up mountains you want to climb but never will.

11. Pore over guidebooks and plan future climbing trips.

12. Watch climbing videos on YouTube or Vimeo.

# Rappelling Tips

## 93. How to Rappel Safely

I've been climbing for a long time, but rappelling still scares me half to death occasionally. For me, it's the least pleasant part of the whole climbing experience. It's also one of the most dangerous, so I like to think that my fears aren't entirely unfounded. A lot of "climbing" accidents happen while rappelling.

There are a number of things you can do to make sure you rappel safely. Make sure your anchors are solid. Make sure your harness is properly secured. Make sure your belay loop is in good shape. Make sure the rope is in good shape (no core shots or anything). Make sure the carabiner of your rappel device is locked. Make sure both sides of the rope are properly threaded through your rappel device and locked into the carabiner. Make sure the knot used to tie the ropes together is set tight and that there is enough tail length. Make sure the rope(s) is (are) long enough to reach the ground or the next rappel station. Tie a stopper knot in the ends of the rope(s) so you don't rappel off the ends. Have your partner double-check your setup before you go on rappel and vice versa.

You can also always use one of the many methods of backing up the rappel (e.g., a prusik knot) so that if you let go of the rope, you won't lose control. I personally very rarely do this, but it's something you can do if rappelling makes you uncomfortable, if you're injured, or if you're rappelling with a heavy pack or haul bag.

## 94. How to Safely Hang Hands-Free While Rappelling

You occasionally might want to stop mid-rappel to take a picture, untangle the ropes, admire a nearby crack, or a number of other things. One quick and simple way to safely do this is to wrap both strands of the free (down) end of the rope around your thigh several times. Usually three of four wraps are enough, though you might need to do more depending on the diameter of your rope and how much friction your rappel device generates.

## 95. Rappelling With a Heavy Backpack or Haul Bag

I don't know if you've ever tried rappelling with a heavy pack on your back, but it sucks. The weight pulls you backward, and fighting to stay upright is a real workout for your neck and abs. The solution? Hang the bag off of your harness's belay loop, as shown in Figure 21.

In the photo, I've girth-hitched a 24-inch (60-centimeter) sling to my belay loop and then clipped the backpack onto that sling. I've tried using a quickdraw before, but it just wasn't long enough for my liking. Your mileage may vary.

Note that I have the carabiner clipped not only into the haul loop on the pack but also through one of the shoulder straps. It's a huge fear of mine (though somewhat unfounded, since I've never heard of it happening before) that the haul loop will rip out, sending my backpack to a sudden and violent death far below. The shoulder strap provides a backup.

It's much, much easier to rappel this way rather than having the bag on your back. You barely feel it there, and you're not being pulled backward or upside down.

*Figure 21. Rappelling with a heavy pack hanging from the belay loop (Tip #95)*

# 96. Tips for Those Free-Hanging Rappels

Most of the time, a rappel is a rappel. But free-hanging rappels are a bit different. Because your feet aren't up against the wall, there's a lot less friction; you slide down the rope faster. There are some things you should be aware of that can make your free-hanging rappels a better experience.

A lot of belay/rappel devices have a high-friction side and a low-friction side. With free-hanging rappels I like to rappel with the down end of the ropes going over the high-friction side of the rappel device. I'd rather go down a rope too slow than too fast. For the first half of the rappel, you may need to manually feed the rope through the device a little bit, but after that it runs smoothly.

Wearing a glove on your break hand can be a lifesaver on any long rappel or when dealing with free-hanging rappels on skinny ropes.

# 97. The Fireman's Belay

The fireman's belay is a rappel backup, but one that you don't need any other gear for. A person at the bottom of the rope holds the rope in his/her hands while the rappeller comes down. If the rappeller loses control and goes too fast, the person at the bottom pulls the ropes tight. This has the same effect as the rappeller pulling back tight on the rope with his/her break hand. Figure 22 illustrates the setup.

I often use the fireman's belay when rappelling with inexperienced rappellers. Because it requires no extra gear or setup, it's something you can do whenever you deem necessary.

*Figure 22. The fireman's belay (Tip #97)*

# Other Tips

# 98. 11 Things All Climbers Should Have in Their Cars

We climbers travel to some pretty far-flung places. If our cars give out on us at inopportune times, we could be in real trouble. Here are some things that every climber should have in his or her car before heading out into the great unknown:

**1. A full tank of gas** – Famous last words: "Dude, relax. I just want to see what's in that next canyon over there." Before you go on any trip, have a full tank of gas. There's no reason not to. This way, you'll find that hidden boulder field and be able to make it back to tell the tale and win the glory.

**2. Paper towels and toilet paper** – For cleaning things, wiping up spills, and doing your business.

**3. Water** – Dying of thirst would be a lousy way to go. Make sure it doesn't happen to you by having a bare minimum of one liter of water in your car per person at all times in addition to whatever you need for climbing. In summer, take more. One time my tires actually caught on fire because I was riding the breaks too hard while coming down a steep mountain road, and I was really happy to have that water in the car.

**4. Warm clothing** – When you're not alpine climbing and worrying about every ounce, you can afford to bring a big, warm jacket. Toss in a wool blanket or sleeping bag and you're even better prepared for cold temperatures.

**5. Flashlight or headlamp** – As a climber, you'll probably already have a headlamp around, but it's not a bad idea to have another one (or a flashlight) in your glove compartment at all times. Spare batteries are also a good idea.

**6. Money** – Hide a few $20 bills under the floor mats or in the glove compartment in case you lose your wallet somewhere and need food or gas.

**7. Jumper cables (and maybe a battery jumper pack)** – Jumper cables alone are OK if there will be other people where you're climbing, but they won't do you much good when your battery has died halfway out to that remote desert tower, will they? You can buy battery jumper packs that are essentially small batteries with jumper cables on them. If you do get one of these, make sure it's fully charged before you head out on that epic adventure.

**8. Spare tire and jack** – First, know how to change a tire. Second, have a spare tire. Third, make sure the spare tire has air in it. Consider keeping a pump or air compressor in the car just in case. I also always have a can or two of that Fix-a-Flat stuff.

9. **Maps** – Get a good state road atlas to supplement your GPS. Printing off good maps from a computer is also an option.

10. **First aid kit** – It doesn't have to be super comprehensive; some Band-Aids, moist towelettes, ibuprofen, tape, gauze, scissors, and antibacterial cream are good for a start.

11. **Spare key** – I was once alone in Dinosaur National Monument, a very remote park in eastern Utah and western Colorado, when I locked my keys in the car. After seeing what I'd done, I started looking around for a rock to smash a window with before thankfully realizing that I had a spare key hidden under my car. Crisis averted.

**Other things** – Maybe a AAA membership? Extra food? Matches? Music? Batteries?

# 99. 12 Ways to Sleep Better When Camping

I hate camping. Whenever someone hears this, they stare at me in disbelief. After all, I'm the outdoorsy guy. I like mountains and camp a lot out of necessity, but yes, I generally dislike camping. The main reason is that I just don't sleep well. Even at home in my bed I'm a light sleeper. It doesn't get any better out on hard earth in the middle of the desert. Here are some tips that have helped me sleep better so that I can climb better the next day (some of these are applicable only to drive-up car camping instead of backpacking):

1. **Use a pillow** – Don't just use a rolled-up jacket. Use a real, honest-to-goodness pillow.

2. **Use a cot or air mattress** – I sleep on my stomach. This makes sleeping on a foam sleeping pad, even a fat one, an unpleasant experience. In the past I used a cot, and that was great. I recently bought a twin-sized air mattress that just barely fits into my tent, and it's amazing. On cold nights, it's still necessary to put a sleeping pad or other insulation on top of the cot or air mattress. They're comfortable but don't provide much insulation by themselves.

3. **Match gear with temperatures** – If it's going to be freezing outside, bring a warm sleeping bag. If it's going to be really hot and humid, don't bring a single-walled tent that doesn't breathe well.

4. **Climb hard the day before** – You'll be able to sleep better if you're tired, and you'll be tired if you climb hard.

5. **Drug yourself** – I've never done this, but apparently taking some NyQuil or

sleeping pills will help you sleep better. One time I was camping near Moab in winter and was in my tent for 14 hours straight (from 6:00 p.m. to 8:00 a.m.) because it was dark outside that whole time. I would have loved a sleeping pill then.

**6. Sleep alone... or with someone** – Some people just don't sleep well when in a confined space with another person. If that's you, bring your own tent instead of sharing. On the other hand, some people can't sleep unless they're next to someone else. Do whatever works for you.

**7. Pick a good spot for your tent** – Pick a dry spot. Pick a level spot (I personally hate sleeping with my head downhill). Pick a spot that doesn't have lots of big rocks or sticks. Pick a spot that won't turn into a pond or river if it rains.

**8. Pick a lonely spot** – Don't camp right next to other people. Other people are loud and annoying and will stay up all night talking. Or they'll blast their music and have a sweet party that you're not invited to. Neither situation is very conducive to a good night's sleep.

**9. Go to the bathroom** – Do your necessary business before you crawl into your tent and sleeping bag. Nothing is worse than waking up in the middle of a freezing cold night and having to pee. Consider bringing a pee bottle into the tent with you so you don't have to venture outside.

**10. Watch what you eat** – Some people can't sleep well right after eating, while others sleep better with a full stomach. Do whatever works for you. Avoid consuming caffeine or high amounts of sugar.

**11. Deaden your senses** – Sleep with earplugs in your ears and a sleep mask over your eyes.

**12. Sleep in your vehicle** – I've found sleeping in my SUV vastly superior to sleeping in a tent. It's way more comfortable. If your vehicle is big enough, spend the night in it.

# 100. Aiding Off of Two Cam Lobes

Sometimes cracks are shallow or flare outward, and you'll find that you can only get half of a cam's lobes in contact with the rock. It's scary to put your weight on one of these placements, but you'd be amazed at how much weight just two cam lobes in contact with the rock can hold.

Consider trying this out at ground level at your local crag first. Place a cam with two lobes touching the rock inside a crack, clip your aiders in, and gingerly test the placement. I've placed cams like this on free routes, but only when nothing else would have worked. It could be just the thing you need when aid

*Figure 23. A cam with only two lobes meaningfully in contact with the rock (Tip #100)*

climbing.

Figure 23 shows a cam with only two lobes (the two deepest in the crack) in meaningful contact with the rock.

# 101. 8 Reasons Your Climbing Photos Suck

Climbing is a very photogenic sport, but that doesn't mean that every climbing photo turns out well. In fact, most climbing photos are pretty bad. Here's why:

**1. The butt shot** – This is the king of bad climbing photos because it's so common. A butt shot is a photo of a climber taken by the belayer (or someone near the belayer) where the most prominent thing in the photo is the climber's butt. No one really wants to see your butt hanging out of its harness, especially if you're stemming or in some other equally unflattering pose. On top of that, butt shots never do the climb or the cliff justice because the climbs always look shorter and less impressive than they really are.

**2. Blurriness** – It can be hard to keep your break hand on the rope and keep your other hand steady enough to take a picture. If you can, steady the camera against something solid like the rock or your head. Better yet, have someone else snap the photo.

3. **Not enough light** – You can't always control how much light you've got, but you can control exposure times or lighten up photos or shadows in photo editing software.

4. **Too much light** – Too much light washes out the photo and can make it difficult to see what's going on.

5. **Toproping** – Pictures of people toproping are just not exciting or interesting. The exception is if you're taking a picture of your second coming up toward you on a multi-pitch route. Those photos can turn out great. But I guess that'd be classified more as following than toproping...

6. **Stupid stuff** – While I'm sure you had a fantastic time back at camp, no one wants to see that pic of your friend with water coming out of his nose. Also, don't tilt the camera to make the route look steeper than it is.

7. **Nothing interesting** – If you're going to take a picture of something and put it on Facebook, at least make sure that something interesting is in the photo. Photos taken from the base of a route looking up are often uninteresting (though they can be valuable for beta purposes) because there's no sense of scale. Photos of your buddy standing at the base of the route are also usually uninspiring.

8. **Other people** – Try not to let other people crash your photos. It's cool seeing you on your sick new proj. But seeing you on your sick new proj with some punk kid flipping off the camera while toproping in the background isn't so cool.

# The End

Thanks for reading this far! I hope you found some useful stuff in here. If you liked this book, please give it a good rating and review on Amazon. Reviews are tremendously beneficial for independent authors and go a long way toward making affordable books possible.

I'd love to hear your feedback or answer any questions you might have. You can also follow me on Twitter (*@climbingtips*), check out my climbing site at *http://theundercling.com*, and follow along with my other adventures at *http://thealoof.com*.

Thanks again,
Tristan Higbee

# Other Books by the Author

*Everest Pilgrim: A Solo Trek to Nepal's Everest Base Camp and Beyond*

*Himalayan Pilgrim: A Chronicle of Independent Trekking Through Nepal's Less-Traveled Regions*

*Annapurna Pilgrim: A Solo Trek of Nepal's Annapurna Circuit in Winter*

*SUV RVing: How to Travel, Camp, Sleep, Explore, and Thrive in the Ultimate Tiny House*

*Hiking Arches National Park: An Opinionated Guide to the Park's Best Hikes*

\*\*\*

Want a free copy of my *Freestanding Hangboard Plans* ebook? Head over to http://theundercling.com/hangboard and enter in the password *climbingtipsbook*.

Made in United States
Orlando, FL
10 March 2024